Structured Chaos:
The Process of Productivity Advance

Richard Blandy, Peter Dawkins, Ken Gannicott,
Peter Kain, Wolfgang Kasper and Roy Kriegler

Published in conjunction with the Australian Productivity Council
and the National Institute of Labour Studies

Melbourne
Oxford University Press
Oxford   Auckland   New York

OXFORD UNIVERSITY PRESS
Oxford New York Toronto Delhi Bombay Calcutta Madras Karachi Singapore Hong
Kong Tokyo Nairobi Dar es Salaam Cape Town Melbourne Auckland
and associates in
Beirut Berlin Ibadan Nicosia

National Library of Australia
Cataloguing-in-Publication data:
Structured chaos.
   Bibliography.
   Includes index.
   ISBN 0 19 554687 3.
   ISBN 0 19 554688 1 (pbk.).
   1. Industrial productivity — Australia.   2. Labor
   productivity — Australia.   I.   Blandy, Richard, 1938–
338.0994

Edited by Sarah Brenan
Typeset by Post Typesetters, Brisbane, Qld.
Printed by Impact Printing, Melbourne
Published by Oxford University Press, 7 Bowen Crescent, Melbourne
OXFORD is a trademark of Oxford University Press

Contents

List of Contributors   iv
Foreword   v
Preface   vii
1   Ready! Fire! Aim! The Sources
    of Productivity Advance   1
2   The Impact of Government on
    Productivity Advance   18
3   The Effects of Different
    Socio-Economic Environments
    on Technological Change   26
4   The Effects of Market Structures
    on Competitiveness   47
5   The Organization of Work
    and Productivity Advance
    in the Workplace   61
Summary and Conclusions   91
Appendix: Recommended
Research Projects   95
References   101
Index   108

Contributors

RICHARD BLANDY is a Professor of Economics and Director of the National Institute of Labour Studies at the Flinders University of South Australia. He holds a Ph.D. from Columbia University and worked for a number of years in the International Labour Office in Geneva. His interests are labour economics, industrial relations, the economics of education and political economy.

PETER DAWKINS is a Research Fellow in the National Institute of Labour Studies at the Flinders University of South Australia on leave from a lectureship in economics at Loughborough University. He holds an M.Sc. (Econ.) from the University of London. His interests are labour economics, the economics of technological change and macro-economics.

KENNETH GANNICOTT is a Senior Lecturer in Economics in the Department of Economics and Management at the new University College of the University of New South Wales within the Defence Academy, Duntroon. He holds an M.A. from Sussex University and his interests are industrial economics, the economics of education and the economics of technical change.

PETER KAIN is a Research Officer in the National Institute of Labour Studies at the Flinders University of South Australia. He holds a B.Ec. (Hons.) from Flinders University and his interests are labour economics and transport economics.

WOLFGANG KASPER is Professor of Economics and Head of the Department of Economics and Management at the new University College of the University of New South Wales within the Defence Academy, Duntroon. He holds a Ph.D. from Kiel University. His main interests are economic growth, international economics, and industrial economics.

ROY KRIEGLER is a Senior Research Fellow in the National Institute of Labour Studies at the Flinders University of South Australia. He holds a Ph.D. from the University of Melbourne. His main interests are the sociology of work and the sociology of organizations.

Foreword

The Australian Productivity Council is an organization committed to the improvement of Australia's economic performance and quality of life.

As the key to this improvement is continuous advance in levels of productivity, we are obliged to study the underlying factors that hinder or assist such advance.

This book, based on research carried out under the auspices of the Council by the National Institute of Labour Studies, is a valuable and thought-provoking contribution to that study. Its findings will interest the informed layman, people in both public and private enterprises, non-business organizations, politicians, economists and students.

It should therefore find a place in Australia's quest for better ways to compete on world and domestic markets, and thus improve the lot of all Australians.

'If economists come to take a broader view of their subject that takes account of the structure of institutions, and if they can communicate their findings to the intelligent layman, we can get better institutional arrangements and a more productive economy. I really believe that our problems are due in part to the narrow conception of their calling that most economists have had, and to the low priority many have given to communicating with intelligent people outside of the profession.

So I end on the plea that as economists we should take the example of the great economists of the past more seriously, and try like them to write more insightfully and clearly about interactions between the markets and the political and social system.'

Mancur Olson (1984)

Preface

This book arises from two months of hectic work by all the authors, followed by two weeks of revision for publication. We are grateful to the Australian Productivity Council for providing the funding for this research. We hope that the book will stimulate further research in the directions we believe are critical if Australian living standards are to rise once again to the levels that the talents and resources of Australians amply justify.

To a large degree, the experience of the National Institute of Labour Studies (to which four of us belong) has provided much of the authors' optimism about the appropriateness of the directions advocated in this book. The Institute does not enjoy a protected existence, despite its position as a research institute of the Flinders University of South Australia. The University provides rooms and services, but makes no allocation from its budget for the staff and maintenance of the Institute — these are met by membership subscriptions, sales of publications, a (fixed-term) grant from the Australian Bureau of Labour Market Research, and especially from sponsored research contracts. Thus the Institute is an entrepreneurial, self-financed research association located within a centrally-funded University. It has a lean, flat, participative structure and a strong sense of purpose. The entrepreneurial function is shared by all the staff. Tasks are undertaken by teams formed *ad hoc* for each purpose. Management is by 'wandering around'. A number of the staff were 'long-term unemployed' before they were engaged; many have been hired as raw University graduates. Forty per cent of the professional staff are women, including the Deputy Director. In-house electronics are managed by non-graduates who had no knowledge of the area when they were appointed. The secretaries make their own organizational arrangements for dealing with an immense workload and have highly flexible working hours.

The success of these arrangements is attested by a twenty-fold increase in income and employment within the space of five years.

Morale is exceptionally high. This book is dedicated to every one of my colleagues who have proved, not only to me, but to themselves, that 'structured chaos' really works.

Thank you, Nena, for typing the final manuscript; Elmar, for preparing the index; and Sarah for a splendid editing job.

Permission to reproduce tables and figures from the following sources is gratefully acknowledged: Ranftl, R.M., Togna, A.D. and Stahl, M.J., 'Improving R. & D. Productivity', *Research Management*, 20 (1), 1977; Shimonshi, D., 'The Mobile Scientist in the American Instrument Industry', *Minerva*, 8 (1), 1970; Freeman, C., *The Economics of Industrial Innovation*, Frances Pinter, London; Kendrick, J. and Crossman, E., *Productivity in the United States: Trends and Cycles*, Johns Hopkins University Press, Baltimore; Nasbeth, L. and Ray, G.F., *The Diffusion of New Industrial Processes: An International Study*, Cambridge University Press; Organisation for Economic Co-operation and Development, *Positive Adjustment Policies*, OECD, Paris; Wang, K., 'Worker Participation Matrix', *Personnel Practice Bulletin*, 30 (3), 1974. Stubbs, P., *Technology and Australia's Future: Industry and International Competitiveness*, Australian Industry Development Association Research Centre, Melbourne.

Richard Blandy

1 Ready! Fire! Aim! The Sources of Productivity Advance

For a century Australia has been going backwards in the international league tables of comparative living standards. From having the highest living standard in the world in the late nineteenth century, we dropped to fourth rank after the Second World War. Since then, the rate of decline has increased. At the beginning of 1985 (before the fall of the Australian dollar on world currency markets) we ranked eighteenth. On present trends, not only will our grandchildren live to be the cheap white trash of Asia, nearly everyone now under 50 will share that experience with them.

These trends in relative living standards reflect underlying trends in international competitiveness. Competitiveness depends on the productiveness of the society, on which depends in turn living standards on the one hand, and costs of production on the other. Highly competitive economies enjoy either high living standards (for example, Switzerland) or low costs of production (as in Hong Kong), or both (as in Japan). Low costs of production can also arise from a low standard of living, which is not an objective of any society. The trick is to have low costs of production together with a high standard of living — to be competitive *at the same time as being well off*. Low costs of production yield expanding market shares for exports and import-competing goods and services, rising living standards and fast economic and employment growth rates. The success of an economy in being able to sustain high and growing living standards (*and* more jobs) depends on sustaining and improving its international competitiveness through fast productivity advance. Australians have, over the past decade, become increasingly aware that their economic growth and productivity levels do not compare favourably with those of other mature industrial economies and that the new industrial countries of Asia are catching up. The 'Lucky Country' attitudes that prevailed in the 1950s and 1960s have given way to a public opinion that is now increasingly alert to a

1

feeling that all is not well in the Australian economy. This change in the public consciousness, brought about by our collective economic experiences since 1973, is a healthy development, providing the springboard for a campaign to raise productivity in every workplace and in the economy as a whole. Creating the right social climate for productivity growth is important because there is no such thing as a productivity gain without sacrifice. In the Australian case, deeply entrenched social arrangements will have to be sacrificed if we are to have faster growth in productivity and job creation, fully utilizing once again the very considerable productive potential that Australia has.

Figure 1 illustrates the well-known fact that Australian economic growth in the post-war period fell short of the growth in per-capita income (and national productivity) in the old industrial

Figure 1 Economic growth: an international comparison

Per capita income
(per capita GDP at 1975 prices and exchange rates)

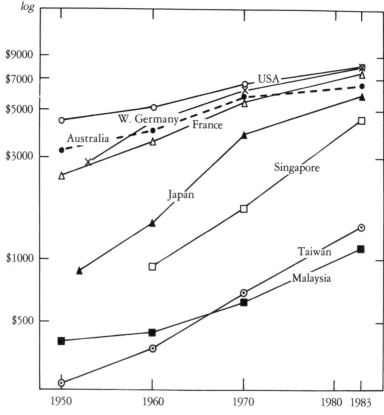

Source: OECD (1983)

countries of the northern hemisphere and the new industrial countries of east Asia. This phenomenon was not limited to the post-war period: growth of per-capita income throughout this century has been comparatively slow in Australia. If these trends were to continue, as we have said, Australia would be among the poorer old industrial countries by the turn of the century and would be surpassed in income (and productivity) levels by the more dynamic societies to our north.

It seems that productivity in manufacturing has been a particular drag on overall productivity levels. Figure 2 shows the results of a comparison of labour productivity levels in 1973 in specific Australian industries with those in the big, advanced industrial economies of Germany and the United States. Although there are severe statistical limitations on comparisons of absolute levels of

Figure 2 The productivity gap: the productivities of Australian industries as a percentage of the average of US and West German productivities

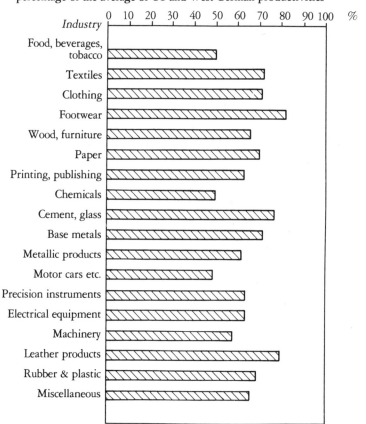

Source: Kasper and Masih (1979)

productivity, one can conclude that Australian productivity levels in most manufacturing industries are 20 to 40 per cent below those of the United States and West Germany, which countries can be taken to represent productivity standards which modern industries can reach. We say 'are' because indications are that there has been no major change since 1973 in the international 'productivity gap' between comparable Australian and leading overseas industries. (A fully-fledged research project could update and refine these comparisons.)*

In the economic debate since the mid-1970s, many observers have argued that Australia's economic malaise and unemployment could be overcome by reducing wage rates. It has been widely claimed that there is a 'wages overhang' which makes many Australian producers uncompetitive both in international markets and — against imports — in domestic markets. This view seems, however, to overlook the important fact that what matters for international competitiveness is the cost level, which is made up of wages and other costs *relative to productivity levels*. If one takes relatively low Australian productivity levels into account, one has to come to the conclusion that there is not so much a 'wages overhang' as a 'productivity underhang'. It is insufficient productivity that deprives many of our industries of their international competitiveness.

Apart from taking a fuller account of the relevant variables, the idea of a 'productivity underhang' leads economic policy onto a socially much more desirable path. The implication of the 'wages overhang' view is that wages and hence incomes must be cut back. This is scarcely an inspiring objective on which to try to build a social consensus to attack our economic problems. By contrast, the view that our productivity requires a boost sets us a constructive task in which all can join, and inspires economic policy with social optimism. The task of raising productivity is of course not easy, and cannot be achieved by a few 'quick fixes'. It will require a persistent, wide-ranging effort to make our society more productivity-conscious and more productivity-oriented. Such changes take time and will affect many diverse aspects of economic and social life. Yet without such adjustments we may have to face the prospect of having changes to our way of life imposed upon us in a more abrupt and painful way later.

To discover what needs to be done to correct Australia's productivity underhang requires a deep understanding of the fundamen-

---

*Possible research projects are suggested at various points in the text: these are drawn together, and in some cases elaborated on, in the Appendix.

tal sources of productivity growth — the socio-economic structures and attitudes which govern the rate of innovation in the economy. This is a very difficult task. Until recently economics was dominated by a mechanical and mathematical analysis of economic growth based on an assumption of complete knowledge (including knowledge of the future) and concentrating on the direct relationship between measured physical inputs and outputs. This approach has provided only a very limited understanding, if any at all, of the problem of how to increase the rate of productivity advance.

Now, a more enlightening set of economic ideas which returns to (and builds on) older, less-quantified analyses of productivity advance has started to develop. In this approach, uncertainty (especially about the future), structures (of markets, of the organization of enterprises, of labour-management relations and of political intervention), and processes (how people do things together) are the key concerns. The focus is essentially on the *social processes* involved in innovation and strong productivity performance.

Dynamic performance is a consequence of how people behave, not, fundamentally, of capital, or technology or plans. The latter follow as a *consequence* of dynamic behaviour by people, not as a cause of people's behaviour.

The ultimate sources of productivity advance, it is now realized, lie in social arrangements. It is true that productivity advance requires technological and organizational improvements, capital and skill accumulation, innovation and reallocations of resources from less to more productive uses. A study of the relationships between these inputs and productivity growth, while illuminating in some respects, still fails to answer the question 'why?'. We know that these things contribute importantly to productivity advance. Why, then, can we not organize ourselves so that we achieve whatever rate of productivity advance we desire, within feasible limits? The answer is that what is feasible within each society or enterprise is determined by the social arrangements regulating that society or enterprise. To improve our rate of technological advance, our rate of innovation, our rate of capital accumulation *requires changes in our social arrangements*. This will require a massive effort. It may not, in fact, be achievable.

We have subtitled this book *The Process of Productivity Advance* because productivity advance emerges as a result of social *processes* which govern our capacity to enhance the more proximate 'sources' of productivity. The main intellectual task in raising Australia's rate of productivity advance is, therefore, to understand these processes and their effects on productivity. Support for this view comes from conventional and radical economists, from industrial sociologists and psychologists, and from leading business consultants and businessmen. See, for example, Nelson (1981), Klein (1977), Weisskopf, Bowles and Gordon (1983), and Peters and Waterman (1983).

In recent years, economists of many ideological persuasions have become convinced that high levels of productivity are dependent on 'hearts and minds', rather than on hardware and capital. For example, the radical American economists Weisskopf, Bowles and Gordon (1983), argue that the slowdown in US productivity growth is only a 'mystery' from the viewpoint of conventional economic analysis which 'neglects the human dimensions of production and the institutional contexts within which economic actors operate' (p. 382). They argue that the reasons for the slowdown are an erosion (since the mid-1960s) of worker co-operation and worker effort, associated with increasing workplace friction, on the one hand, and a decline in business innovation over the same period, on the other. From the perspective presented here, these two factors are related. From a different ideological perspective, the management consultants, Peters and Waterman (1983, p. 238) urge managers to:

> ... Treat people as adults. Treat them as partners; treat them with dignity; treat them with respect. Treat *them* — not capital spending and automation — as the primary source of productivity gains. These are fundamental lessons learned from the excellent companies research ...

Richard Nelson (1981, p. 1036) argues:

> The social system of work sets norms, enforces them, and resists pressures or commands from management that are inconsistent with those norms ... How workers feel about their job, about fellow workers, about management, and about the organisation, may be more important in influencing productivity than is the particular way they are instructed to do their work, the formal organisational structure, or even financial incentives ...

Finally, Professor Sir Henry Phelps-Brown (1977) argues that the decline in Britain's relative position with the rest of the world cannot be corrected while class antagonism persists and is expressed through the industrial relations system. He argues that cultural attitudes and values are the critical factors for a country's dynamic success (or otherwise) in the economic sphere.

These ideas are compelling, in our opinion, in providing understanding of the problem. If there is one book which best conveys the flavour of what is involved, it is Peters and Waterman's analysis of what distinguishes the best companies in the United States from their rivals: *In Search of Excellence.*

What Peters and Waterman show over and over again is the importance of human attitudes and values and institutional arrangements in determining whether organizations are excellent, high productivity places — or not. Those messages can be extended to the society at large. What matters, at every stage, is the capacity of the society to thrive on change rather than to frustrate it, to be adaptable and flexible rather than fixed in ways of going about things, to be innovative and adventurous rather than seeking protection and an illusory certainty. To foster successful traits for productivity advance, societies need to provide incentives, that is, rewards, for demonstrating those traits, and institutional arrangements which will permit productive traits to flower. This is not an issue of monetary rewards — although monetary reward structures may be important. It is essentially a matter of hearts and minds, of human attitudes and values and institutions.

In fact, this 'new' message is not really new at all. It is a rediscovery, a re-evaluation, of lessons developed by economists over the past 200 years, but lost sight of in the desire to construct a mechanical view of how economies work. For example, Alfred Marshall, Professor of Economics at Cambridge University at the turn of the century and one of the most famous economists who ever · lived, wrote in the preface to his *Principles of Economics:*

> The main concern of economics is thus with human beings who are impelled, for good and evil, to change and progress. Fragmentary statical hypotheses are used as temporary auxiliaries to dynamical — or rather biological — conceptions: but the central idea of economics ... must be that of living force and movement.

The world of dynamic analysis is one of *uncertainty.* New happenings occur persistently *but unpredictably* as a result of the competitive rivalries of nations, enterprises, unions, individuals, and organizations generally. Many prices, costs, production processes and products are *not* known, in particular because they are constantly changing in unpredictable ways or by unpredictable degrees as a result of changing patterns of human endeavour.

In such a world, entrepreneurs, innovators and inventors are central figures, who lead the social discovery processes by which prices, costs, processes and products can be unearthed — the processes by which organizations and societies are able to adapt and cope and compete with the rivals surrounding them and with the risks each imposes on the others. Large-scale production units offer less advantage in such a world because the capacity laid down may rapidly become obsolete as a result of changing demand patterns, costs and technologies. Flexibility in meeting unpredictable changes becomes critical for survival and prosperity, because the world is characterized by such changes.

Organizational complexities and inflexibilities associated with large-scale units increase the costs and difficulties of adapting to change and, therefore, smaller-scale organizations possess considerable advantages in a rapidly changing world. The ability of workers at all levels to adapt to changing circumstances and to create changes conferring a competitive edge on their organizations becomes a substantial economic advantage. Lateral consultation between semi-autonomous groups co-operating in common endeavours is, we would claim, more effective in getting things done than pyramidical command structures. In this scheme planning is confined to broad objectives shared and understood by the various semi-autonomous units. Important values for a society inhabiting a dynamically changing world include creativity, autonomy, co-operativeness, tolerance, simplicity, openness, trust, optimism, power-sharing and an urge to action. The industrial relations system consistent with this environment would emphasize worker participation, resolution of disputes by conciliation among the parties directly involved, workplace consultation and bargaining, and a diffusion of managerial prerogatives to the whole work group.

There are some real economies that possess, or have possessed, these characteristics to such degree that they have prospered in recent times — for example, Japan.

The Tokyo correspondent of the *Australian Financial Review*, drawing on five years of experience in Tokyo, has summed up his understanding of the reasons for the success of the Japanese in the following way:

> ... Japan's comparative advantage is in speed, flexibility, a thoroughly dedicated and capable workforce, and the sheer ambition to win at whatever it is doing.
>
> This makes static Japanese blueprints suspect: they are not where the action is...
>
> Contrary to what seems to be the general expectation in

Australia, Japan almost certainly has no firm blueprint to where it is going, nor are even the most important developments in Japan orchestrated from a position of great organisation.

Japan is chaotic; but, more importantly, miraculously Japan manages to usually produce perfect order at the last moment from apparently irretrievable confusion — and to do so in a way which leads it directly to the big time... (Byrnes, 1984, p. 11)

Productivity advance in a rapidly changing world requires social arrangements which have *evolutionary capacity*, a capacity to accommodate the unforeseen and unforeseeable, a capacity to sail on the shifting socio-economic winds rather than trudging relentlessly on with fixed structures to ultimate defeat in an increasingly hostile environment.

Organizations and societies not adapted to dynamic performance in a changing world will have high labour productivity and competitiveness only while the initial circumstances to which they are adapted persist. As conditions change, inability to adapt flexibly and efficiently will erode the initial advantages of such organizations and societies, compared with their more dynamically-adapted rivals. Further, attempts to maintain existing structures through protective interventions by governments and their authorities have the unfortunate consequence of reducing the incentive for organizations to retain flexibility and capacity to cope with uncertainty. As is well known, the greater the degree of 'insurance' provided against losses resulting from the occurrence of unfavourable (but uncertain) events, the less is the incentive for the 'insured' to make provision to cope themselves with such eventualities. In a world of 100 per cent 'insurance', for example, it would be inefficient for the insured to devote any resources to avoiding insurable losses. Losses from adverse events are then most efficiently met by simply making claims on the 'insurance policies' offered by the 'insurance' authorities, i.e. governments and their agencies. Thus, the more interventionist governments become in 'protecting' organizations from the need to adapt as circumstances alter, the more bureaucratized and inflexible organizations will become, which makes them even less able to cope with uncertainty. They may, in fact, become incapable of dealing with new circumstances. Their productivity and competitiveness will fall. The massive extent of government regulation and protection of established industries and producers (public and private) in Australia is a fundamental reason for our low rate of productivity advance and loss of international competitiveness.

As conditions change, the dynamically adapted societies overtake their sluggish, inflexible rivals in productivity and competitiveness: Rabbits 1, Dinosaurs 0. The same is true — or should be true — of individual enterprises within any society. A high degree of competitive rivalry between producers is, therefore, a further important ingredient in the structure of dynamically successful economies. The higher the degree of competitive interaction between organizations, the more uncertainty there will be in the environment, the more favourable will be the incentives for entrepreneurship and innovation to meet the risks imposed by rivals, and the more rapid will be the rate of growth of productivity and competitiveness. The more uncertainty in the environment, the less the degree of bureaucracy that societies should impose on their institutions and the less the degree of bureaucracy that institutions and organizations should impose on their members. There is an optimal degree of bureaucratization ('structure') and an optimal degree of 'openness' (willingness to alter what is done and the way things are done) corresponding to every degree of uncertainty in the environment (Klein, 1977, p. 174).

Apart from the adverse dynamic consequences of government interventions designed to protect established interests, and of market structures which limit rivalry between producers, of crucial concern is the nature of *organizational structures* and their effects on entrepreneurship, technological change and innovation. Klein (p. 161) makes some telling observations on this matter:

> ... Another important difference between organisations optimised for a high degree of dynamic efficiency and those optimised for a high degree of static efficiency* is that the former tend to contain more trust than the latter. This occurs because the role relationships are looser — and the looser the role relationships, the wider the latitudes in which people trust each other. In fact, all inventive behaviour can be regarded as an externality that depends upon trust ... It must be emphasised, however, that for trust to exist an organisation must have a genuine sense of mission. ... It is the sense of mission that permits trust to exist and conflict to be of a highly impersonalised nature.
>
> Conversely, in organisations that feature mainly static

---

*Dynamic efficiency (or dynamic capability) is the capacity to economize in the face of economic parameters which are endlessly changing in unpredictable ways; static efficiency is the capacity to economize given economic parameters which are constant and known.

efficiency the relationships between the members of the bureaucracy must be more precisely defined, with the almost inevitable
result that trust is in short supply; that is, people trust each
other within very narrow limits...

Organizations (and societies) with a high degree of bureaucratization, whether they have a sense of purpose or not, are likely to
have low dynamic capability because the diversity of interactions
between members (which leads to new ideas) is restricted, role
relationships are tightly defined, trust is likely to be in short supply
and willingness to experiment and innovate is likely to be subdued
as a result.

Organizations (and societies) with high dynamic capability, on
the other hand, are those with loose organizational structures, but
a strong shared sense of purpose or mission (organized disorgani-
zation or structured chaos). Such organizations achieve consensus
not by imposition from above but by evolution from below. These
organizations also have a strong capacity to cope with uncertainty
by their own resourcefulness. The trust which exists within such
organizations permits more complex innovations to be attempted
(whose effects are more uncertain) than less trusting environments
(Ettlie and Vellenga, 1979). In those organizations, individuals
perform their special tasks in the light of their knowledge of the
tasks of the organization as a whole. Jobs are redefined continually
by interaction with others participating in a task. Interaction runs
laterally as much as vertically. Communication between persons of
different ranks tends to resemble lateral consultation rather than
vertical commands. Omniscience can no longer be imputed to those
at the top (Burns and Stalker, 1961).

It turns out, therefore, that dynamic efficiency, on which fast
productivity growth, high living standards and the maintenance of
international productivity competitiveness depend, is associated, in
theory, with employee participation, in the sense defined by the
Australian Minister for Employment and Industrial Relations, Mr
Willis:

> For Australia to achieve sustained economic recovery and
> growth it is critical that the consensus and co-operation being
> developed at the national level be given practical expression at
> the workplace.
>
> Industrial democracy and employee participation have
> come to mean many things to many people. The essence of
> the issue is simply about employees at all levels in an organi-

sation having greater influence and involvement in their work. Every employee has a right to a high quality of work life and to contribute to the effective operation of the organisation ... (Willis, 1984)

Here, both elements needed for high dynamic capability are stated: consensus (shared objectives) and looseness of structure and role relationships ('employees at all levels having greater influence and involvement in their work').

Alfred Marshall, who was mentioned earlier, drew attention a long time ago to the two-way relationship between efficiency and shared values and trust:

> ... the efficiency of a nation is strengthened by and strengthens the confidences and affections which hold together the members of each economic group — the family, employers and employees in the same business, citizens of the same country ... (Marshall, 1920, p. 38)

In this book we attempt to develop essential aspects of this *theory of the dynamic evolutionary economy*, and to identify critical matters about which more empirical knowledge is required as a basis for action to improve the rate of Australian productivity advance. There seem to us to be four major areas of study essential to a process approach to improving Australia's rate of productivity advance:

1 The impact of government on productivity advance.
2 The effects of different socio-economic environments on techno-logical change.
3 The effects of market structures on competitiveness.
4 The organization of work, and productivity advance in the workplace.

The next four chapters discuss these matters in turn.

Before proceeding with this discussion, it may be helpful to briefly review for the reader what is meant by productivity, and how it is measured. It may seem strange that we have nearly reached the end of the first chapter before doing this. The reason is simple: like 'quality', everyone knows productivity when they see it, but it defies simple measurement. What we are really concerned about *is* the 'productiveness' of the society — its capacity to produce goods and services to satisfy its wants, and/or those of other economies. But tying down this commonsense idea of productiveness is not simple in a complex economy.

Strictly speaking, the definition of productivity is absolutely straightforward. It is simply output per unit of input. For example, if a ditch-digger digs 100 metres of ditch a week, then the productivity of the ditch-digger is 100 metres of ditch per week. If he manages to dig 200 metres of ditch per week his productivity has doubled. Perhaps he did this with a new digging method, or because the ground was softer, or he used better equipment. But, for whatever reason, he has managed to get more output from his work time — to get more for the same (or less). This is the whole idea — our standard of living depends on how much we can produce in a given period of time — the more, the higher our standard of living.

Different measures are relevant for different purposes. Thus, *labour productivity* (defined as output per hour of labour employed) is the relevant concept in considering what rate of increase of the average money wage would be consistent with maintaining constant the share of wages in national income. This rate of increase can be shown in an abstract theoretical way to be the rate of inflation plus the rate of *growth* in labour productivity. But since the real economy consists of millions of products and services, produced by millions of people of diverse characteristics, there is a considerable problem in knowing what weights to assign to each product, service and person in order to derive a proper measure of output and input. In fact, there is no 'scientifically correct' way of doing this independent of further assumptions about how to value these diverse things. Hence, our actual measure can only be an approximate, rough guide.

Similarly, *total factor productivity* is the relevant concept when comparing the productiveness or efficiency with which resources are used in different industries or in the same industry in different countries. The reason for this is that high labour productivity (in the mining industry, say) compared with low labour productivity (in the retail sales sector, say), may be accompanied by low *capital productivity* in the former industry and high capital productivity in the latter. The former industry may be quite wasteful in its use of capital (and the high labour productivity reflects the abundance of capital used by labour in the industry) whereas the latter industry may be very sparing and efficient in its use of capital (and the low labour productivity reflects this lack of capital abundance). A measure of productivity which takes account of different intensities of resource use is relevant in looking at the efficiency of resource use, but the difficulties of weighting each resource are compounded when the number of them is increased. Approximate compromise measures are inevitably adopted, with different measures being adopted by different countries. The sensible approach is to take these measures as rough guides to the theoretical ideas they are trying to capture.

There is, as might now be guessed, a whole family of productivity concepts and measures. The unifying idea behind this diverse family is that of a 'production function'. A production function expresses the fact that the physical volume of output depends on the physical volume of inputs *and* on the efficiency with which they are used. The notion of a production function can range in application from individual firms, to entire industries, to sectoral groups such as manufacturing or primary, and on up to economy-wide measures that relate gross output to all associated inputs.

Only when output is related to all associated inputs, as it is when we measure *total factor productivity*, can we be confident that we are measuring the efficiency with which resources as a whole are being used. It is obvious that measures of total productivity are extremely demanding of data, requiring as they do information on both labour and capital inputs. Even then the result may only be an approximation of the correct total input if, for example, inputs of intangible capital or differences in the quality of labour cannot be measured and included.

Recognition of this problem has provoked some path-breaking work in productivity analysis in the last two decades. We remarked earlier that only if changes in output are related to changes in all associated inputs (total factor productivity) can we determine when there are net savings in inputs and thus any increase in overall productivity. Conversely, we can state that increase in productivity equals that part of the change in output that is not accounted for by measured changes in the inputs. Stated this way, productivity change becomes the *residual* in the calculation of the relationship between inputs and outputs. This residual is sometimes referred to as 'the third factor', meaning everything not explained by the two measurable factors — labour and capital. Clearly, if we only have very crude and simple measures of labour and capital inputs, then the 'residual' or 'third factor' will not be very informative. We shall have measured productivity increase while gaining very little information even about the direct factors associated with that increase. It is for this reason that the 'residual' has been tagged 'a measure of our ignorance'.

The pioneering contributions of Kendrick (1977) and Denison (1967) (among others) have chipped away at this problem, steadily reducing our ignorance of the direct sources of productivity increase. Instead of being limited to crude quantitative measures of labour and capital, it is now possible to measure a wide variety of intangible and qualitative determinants of productivity.

Table 1 shows sources of productivity *growth* in the United States for two periods between 1948 and 1976. (Since we are using this table for purely illustrative purposes, we have deliberately excluded data on the 'productivity slowdown' of the last decade, the sources of which are a matter of contention.) The third line of the table shows that part of the change in output that is not explained by the change in tangible inputs. The rise in total productivity (2.9 and 1.4 percentage points, respectively), has been attributed to seven

Table 1 U.S. domestic business economy, sources of growth of real gross product, contributions to growth in percentage points, 1948–66 and 1966–76

	1948–66	1966–76
Real gross product	3.9	2.8
Tangible factor inputs	1.0	1.4
Total factor productivity	2.9	1.4
Advances in knowledge	1.4	1.1
Formal R&D	.85	.7
Informal	.3	.3
Changes in rate of diffusion	.25	.1
Changes in quality of labor	.6	.5
Education and training	.6	.8
Health and vitality	.1	.1
Age-sex composition	−.1	−.4
Actual/potential efficiency	—	—
Changes in quality of land	—	−.1
Resource reallocations	.3	.1
Self-employment to employment	.1	—
Interindustry labor shifts	.4	.1
Weighting effects	−.2	—
Volume-related factors	.6	−.2
Economies of scale	.5	.3
Intensity of demand	.1	−.5
Irregular factors	—	—
Net government impact	—	−.1
Government services to business	.1	.1
Business services to government	−.1	−.2
Residual factors, n.e.c.	—	.1

Source: Kendrick and Grossman (1980), Table 2.1

main sources: advances in knowledge; changes in the quality of labour; changes in the quality of land (from technical advances in agricultural and mineral industries); resource reallocations (by which is meant the speed with which resources move to higher productivity uses in conformity with community preferences); volume-related factors (including the economies of scale that come with the growth of local, national, and international markets, and changes in the rates of capacity utilization from cyclical factors); net government impact (which measures the contributions of government to business productivity, and, conversely, the impact on business of government reporting requirements and regulations).

The sheer diversity of sources of productivity advance is a striking feature of this table. The sources range from informal inventive activity, to improved health; from economies of scale, to the role of self-employment; and from the quality of land, to the role of government. In fact, as we have argued earlier, the seven categories listed in Table 1 are by no means a definitive list. The seven items are what we may call only the *proximate* determinants of productivity advance. Underlying these proximate determinants are the 'hearts and minds' and the institutional framework of the economy. As Kendrick (1977, p. 70) has noted:

> Institutions are created and evolve within a set of laws and governmental regulations, of course. The legal framework and changes in laws and regulations are particularly important, for they govern the rewards for high and rising productivity and the penalties for sub-normal performance. In a mixed economy ... several kinds of factors have significant impacts on productivity: the rules for the competitive sector and policing under the antitrust laws; the modes of regulating public utilities and other natural monopolies; the nature of interventions in the operation of markets; and social legislation and regulations, among others.

This institutional framework is in turn a function of the basic values of society. By this we mean such things as the desire for material improvement, the willingness to assume responsibility and to take risks, and the readiness to adapt to change. All these things affect productivity.

The overall conclusion that emerges from this survey of definitions and determinants is that practically everything in a modern economy is grist for the productivity mill. Productivity advance is not just worker efficiency in the organization and methods sense: it derives also from the legal framework of society. It is not just the down-to-earth question of economies of scale, but also the very method of regulating monopolies such as airlines and electricity. And it is not just formal advances in technical knowledge, but also the fundamental value system of society which shapes the way in which that knowledge will be put to useful application.

2 The Impact of Government on Productivity Advance

When we talk about the effects of government on productivity, we have made our first move into the difficult area of grappling with basic social values and the institutional framework.

Government regulations

Consider the entries in Table 1 (Chapter 1) for net government impact. These entries measure the positive contributions of government to business productivity and, conversely, the negative impact on business of government requirements and regulations. In the US these two categories were in balance during the 1948–66 period. In the decade from 1966, the average annual increase in costs imposed by environmental, occupational, and health and safety regulations amounted to 0.2 percentage points — sufficient to make the net effect of government a *negative* contribution to productivity growth.

Consider also the strongly negative effect on productivity in 1966–76 of changes in the age–sex composition of the labour force. During this decade, the proportions of women and young people in the labour force rose much faster than in the earlier period. These two groups have relatively little labour force experience, and in the theory underlying these calculations are assumed to have lower productivity than groups with more experience and on-the-job training.

The implications of these results for net government impact and age–sex composition are worth highlighting. It may well be desirable for society to impose environmental, discrimination, health and safety, or affirmative action regulations, or to encourage female participation in the workforce. But the value of Table 1 is that it shows very clearly that such policies may not be free: they can diminish the rate of productivity growth in the economy. An informed society may well feel that that price is worth paying, but this judgement ought to be made in the knowledge of what the price might be.

In this illustration we have concentrated on the possible productivity dimension of social legislation. Phillips (1975, p. 2) has usefully written of the pervasiveness of regulation:

> ... for instance, regulation may be required in the distribution
> of gas and electricity because of economies of scale and the
> existence of 'natural monopolies'; this surely is not the basis for
> regulating the price farmers receive for milk. Regulation of
> radio and television involves licensing and limited control over
> service quality, but essentially no control over pricing. Regula-
> tion of taxi service, on the other hand, involves detailed price
> regulation as well as licensing in some locales, and little regu-
> lation of any kind in others ... The automobile industry (must
> conform to) safety and pollution standards. Meat packing and
> food canning ... are subject to numerous grading, packaging,
> and health regulations. What of the pharmaceutical industry?
> Barbers and beauticians? Operations of private fleets of trucks?

There is at present a substantial debate in Australia about
various aspects of deregulation. Some form of government regulation is often justified on the grounds that a free market does not
allocate resources efficiently. However, in recent years, there has
been increasing recognition, in this country as in others, of two
fundamental problems of regulation. The first is that even if freely
competitive markets do fail from some social point of view (and who
would deny it?), it is pointless contrasting this failure with a
theoretically correct government regulation. The proper procedure,
it is now realized, is to compare market failure with the *reality* of
government intervention. There may be government failure as well
as market failure. The second problem arises from the first: regulation by government can turn out to have unintended and unforeseen consequences. One topical example is the banking system. Until
very recently, Australian banking has been tightly circumscribed by
regulations on deposits, interest rates, and even cheque accounts.
One objective of this regulation has been to help the poor, particularly by low-cost housing funds. Regulation is now widely believed
to have done the opposite, by rationing the supply of funds to the
very people it was supposed to help. Banking regulation not only
failed in its social objective, but also resulted in a less productive
banking system.

The adverse impact of government regulation on productivity
advance, and the positive results of deregulation, are much discussed

in the international research literature. For example, Nelson and Wohar's (1983) study of US electric generation concludes that regulations designed to restrict the growth of power demand also reduced productivity, because productivity is positively related to the level of output. Gollop and Roberts (1983) conclude that sulphur dioxide regulations for US industries reduced the rate of productivity growth. Caves, Christensen and Swanson (1981) examine US and Canadian railroads, where the latter are relatively unregulated on passenger and freight charges. They conclude that this freedom has led to greater efficiency on the Canadian railroads. Similarly, Caves, Christensen and Tretheway (1982) examine the deregulation of airlines in the USA. They find higher productivity has resulted from the freeing of competitive forces. Mescon and Vozikis (1982) concur: to them 'deregulation of industry in the United States has served as a catalyst and revitalisation of small business activity'.

Malkiel (1979) suggests that regulations add uncertainty, costs, risks and delays to the implementation of projects, thus dampening enthusiasm for new investment. McCain (1978) suggests that an alternative to direct regulation, with its undesirable effects, is to control by taxing, e.g. to put a tax (price) on pollution. By *taxing* (pricing), rather than *regulating*, misallocation of resources will be reduced, according to McCain. Taxing is preferable because those whose costs are least affected will stop the offending action; under regulation, the actions that are very costly to stop are treated the same as those that are relatively inexpensive to stop.

Mescon and Vozikis (1982) argue that government regulatory requirements divert management's attention from entrepreneurial drive: product development, production, and marketing concerns. They see the emergence of a risk-avoiding, selfish, listless society. They advocate that *sunrise* legislation should be introduced, requiring regulatory programmes to spell out specific objectives, as well as *sunset* legislation to force parliaments to conduct periodic reviews of regulatory programmes to determine whether or not they have outlived their effectiveness.

Butcher (1979) even argues that most business-funded research and development (R & D) in the USA is to a large degree, 'defensive', i.e. designed to comply with government regulations. Such R & D does virtually nothing for growth. Butcher advocates, therefore, that regulation legislation include (1) economic impact statements of regulations, and (2) a goals-oriented approach to regulations (as advocated also by Mescon and Vozikis). Each regulation should say not how to do things, but what the regulation is setting out to achieve. Administrators and markets should then solve the problem of how to meet the objective.

The massive growth in regulations over the past twenty years has much increased 'system risks' to business, that is, the systemic risk of future change to the social environment for which enterprise plans. A growing and more activist bureaucracy introduces more frequent changes to the business environment, often without knowing the full consequences of these new initiatives, especially on productivity advance.

A favourable 'climatic' factor would be created if it was more widely realized that firms are helped by a steady government policy environment and that activist governments (no doubt with the best of intentions) disrupt long-term investment plans of firms by their frequent stop-go actions. Simple and stable regulations seem to be important. Most entrepreneurs (especially in smaller firms which often are the key to job-creation and innovation) tend to be irritated by the need to learn and re-learn a vast array of rules and regulations that they consider peripheral to their firm's purpose. The successful may even succeed by ignoring or not investing the time and trouble to learn this mass of ever-changing rules. A better understanding is needed by all government institutions that there is a need for a stable underlying order for enterprise, innovation and productivity advance to flourish. 'Order' in this sense is the order which Ortega y Gasset meant when he wrote in 1927 that 'order is not a pressure imposed ... from without, but an equilibrium which has grown from within'.

A much-needed research study is a survey of Australian firms to discover the effect regulations have on them, focusing on prospects for raising productivity which firms have failed to pursue because of regulations. Such a survey of productivity-inhibiting regulations would reveal which sorts of regulations are problems and which are not.

In an example of how regulation can inhibit innovation, Johnson and Pikarsky (1984) have outlined the growth of technical and service innovations for Chicago public transportation in the years 1880 to 1930. Those years were characterized by limited — and, especially, fragmented — regulation by state, district and park authorities. An often-proposed strategy for stimulating efficient transportation is to co-ordinate and consolidate services. The tightened rope of regulation after 1930 had such an impact. However, the scale of innovation witnessed in the years prior to 1930 disappeared. The period 1880 to 1930 had witnessed the evolution of transportation from horse-drawn trams to cable cars, steam-powered 'rapid transit' lines, electric trams, motor buses, trolley buses and jitneys. The subsequent fifty years, with public-sector control and 'co-ordination', has witnessed few, if any, comparable innovations. Johnson and Pikarsky conclude that competition is required to stimulate innovation: duplication of service, resulting from competition, far from being inefficient, as the bureaucrat's manuals say, has

> had the very beneficial effect of keeping transportation operators 'tuned in' to changing consumer needs. It has the very healthy effect of a steady introduction of innovation ... Consolidation has contributed to reducing a once vibrant, albeit chaotic, industry to a lumbering, moribund giant which has little relevance to the way we live today.

The authors call for a deregulated system, enabling competition and a subsequent innovative response to change. Specifically, they advocate fragmentation of transport systems and a chaotic but highly innovative service, in lieu of a consolidated, moribund, public monolith.

This is a splendid example, in our view, of the way social arrangements affect productivity advance. As we will show at some length later, 'planning', 'co-ordination', 'elimination of duplication and overlap' and the pursuit of 'economies of scale' (all favourites in the bureaucratic lexicon) appear to have very adverse consequences for productivity advance. The emerging, preferable set of arrangements is best described as 'structured chaos'.

A second useful research project, therefore, is a series of case studies of strongly regulated activities that would analyse the contribution of regulation/deregulation to productivity in Australia. An approximation to this sort of study was done by the Brookings Institution in the United States, examining regulation in domestic airlines, surface freight, ocean freight, electric power generation and supply, inter-city telecommunications, car insurance, the stock exchange, and savings banks. An incidental advantage of such a series is that it could correct the frequent worry that deregulation is a 'leap in the dark'. Existing regulations set out certain, specific requirements for an industry, whereas deregulation may appear to offer merely the unknown and unpredictable workings of a free market. The Brookings Institution was able to spell out what the efficiency and social consequences of deregulating the various industries were likely to be.

Regulation is not the only way in which governments may affect productivity, however.

Government ownership

Caves and Christensen's (1980) study of the efficiency of government-owned Canadian National (railway) relative to private Canadian Pacific (railway) concluded that public ownership was not inherently less efficient than private ownership. However, Kain (1981) showed that public takeover of Adelaide's private bus network led to a substantial fall in productivity. Further, the foray of Australia's East-West Airline into the government-enforced Ansett Airlines/TAA duopoly suggests that the 'two-airline policy' is inefficient, with the impact of public ownership possibly being masked under the overall policy arrangements.

Globerman and Smart (1983) argue that efficiency has also suffered from the growth of government through the migration of workers from the 'productive' private sector to the 'unproductive' public sector. This shift exacerbates the adverse productivity consequences which arise if there is a lack of opportunity for productivity improvement in public services. To quote Hanlon (1981) on this point, 'the major barrier to the use of technological innovation for improving productivity is that many public services do not allow for a "technological fix"', for example, recreation, social welfare, and education services. He argues that where the possibilities for technological innovation are limited in public services, productivity improvement, viewed in the broad sense of organizational effectiveness, must amount to the 'creative and sensitive management of human resources'. He suggests that labour-management projects recently undertaken in the public sector in the USA have the dual objective of improving productivity and quality of life. He concludes, however, that there is no universal principle that ensures that increasing employees' job satisfaction will result in higher productivity. Quoting other researchers, Hanlon says that improving job attitudes and productivity at the same time is more difficult than improving job attitudes alone. However, the realization of both objectives is also more dependent upon better management of human resources than upon greater capital investment or technological innovation.

There are two areas for further research which could be considered here. First, studies could be undertaken of the productivity performance of Australian publicly-owned enterprises, either in comparison with private enterprises in Australia or with similar publicly-owned or private enterprises in other countries. Second, studies could be made of the potential productivity gains in the public sector resulting from a greater rate of technological innovation and from adopting different work organization strategies (see Chapter 5).

Government actions enhancing productivity

The research literature on the effect of government on productivity advance does not simply emphasize the detrimental impact of government intervention on productivity. There is also the traditional emphasis on *positive* government action to correct market failure, or arguments for government policy to be altered to 'the social benefit' in various ways.

Collins (1981), for instance, discusses various tax incentives for innovation. Malkiel (1979) argues for major tax changes to encourage the undertaking of long-term risks, and to shift investment incentives 'away from real estate (tax) shelters and municipal bonds and toward capital formation'.

Boretsky (1980) calls for the lengthening of the time horizon of economic policy-making, to allow time for the introduction of successful technological change, for example. Policy should not be just directed at the management of currently available productive resources, but also at the development of new and more efficient productive resources. Government policy should be formulated the way good business is managed: successful business leaders have long-term strategies and efficiency-oriented investment policies rather than emphasizing short-term cash flow considerations. Economic policy makers, to be successful, should learn from this.

Salomon (1980) suggests government assistance is necessary to promote technological change and to reverse the declining rate of economic growth in the US. He questions whether we can expect recovery in demand to stimulate technical change when inadequate technical change may itself be one of the long-term sources of stagnation.

On this point, Sahal (1983) argues that if there is to be any planning of productivity growth, then a policy of 'balanced growth' is wrong. Given that a handful of industries account for a disproportionately large part of total productivity growth, says Sahal, the objective of policy should be to promote growth of the few leading sectors. These sectors would then propel the stagnant sectors forward. Thus a policy of lopsided growth will, he claims, achieve more than balanced growth; a balanced growth policy is ineffectual at best and counter-productive at worst. Against this we would point out that a strategy of 'picking the winners' is difficult in a world which is essentially and always full of uncertainties. There is much evidence that no one can pick the winners with certainty (least of all governments) and that the best strategy is to stimulate *the number of experiments and attempts being undertaken,* to encourage those that prove to be winners and to discourage those that prove to be losers. Policies that work through market processes are more likely to be able to accomplish the last of these objectives than direct government involvements are (see Klein, 1977; Peters and Waterman, 1983; Schultze, 1983).

A research project which could be considered here is to investigate what changes in taxation and subsidies and direct government support would most stimulate overall productivity advance by increasing the number of new products and processes being developed in the economy as a whole. (See Chapter 3 on the connection between innovation and productivity advance.) Note that this includes failures as well as successes: the number of successes can only be achieved by increasing the number of failures as well, since if we knew which was which in advance we would never have a failure. No one deliberately sets out to create a failure. The number of attempts at developing new products and processes appears to be the critical factor.

Other interesting research would be to examine what changes in the structure of policy-making, and in the political system more generally, would induce a longer-term focus to economic policy, more conducive to policy measures to facilitate long-term productivity advance, rather than measures to gain immediate political advantage.

3 The Effects of Different Socio-Economic Environments on Technological Change

There is no neat, completely general definition of the concept of 'technological change'. Many authors do not attempt to define it at all. Rather they prefer to proceed into discussion and analysis of it without worrying about a definition (e.g., Nelson, 1981). Here we adopt a definition which would seem to be implied in the common usage of the term and in much of the literature. *Technological change* 'is the process by which economies change over time in respect of the products they produce and the processes used to produce them' (Stoneman, 1983, p. 3). For the purposes of this book, which is built around the concept of productivity advance, we go on to define *technological progress* as productivity-enhancing changes in products or processes resulting from improvements in knowledge (invention), their application (innovation), or diffusion.

We take the concept of technological change (or progress) to be different from the concept of organizational change (or progress), though they overlap. *Organizational progress* is defined as productivity-enhancing changes resulting from changes in the organization of production, (e.g., management structures, industrial relations system, payment systems, ownership and control, etc.). Organizational progress is taken up in Chapter 5.

In the real world, technological change and organizational change are hard to disentangle. Indeed, we will go on to argue that they are inextricably linked and should be considered jointly in the analysis of productivity advance. Meanwhile we treat them as different, but overlapping, which is in keeping with much of the literature. For the moment we are concerned with technological change.

The process of technological change can be divided into three phases: invention, innovation and diffusion. *Invention* is the first appearance of a novel idea; *innovation* is the first commercial application of an invention; and *diffusion* is the pattern of adoption of an innovation by users. A distinction may also be made between basic inventions, which are of largely scientific interest, and applied inventions, with immediate practical application in industry or commerce, (Bosworth, 1983b).

Measuring technological progress

Technological changes can be measured in a number of ways. The measures can, however, be divided into two types — input and output measures. The most usual *input* measure is expenditure on research and development (R & D). The most usual *output* measure is the rate of patenting activity.

Spending on R & D is an input to both invention and innovation, and innovation is at the heart of the process of technological change. Hence, a high level of expenditure on R & D might be regarded as implying rapid innovation and technological progress. But a direct connection between these is not easy to establish. Gibson (1976) argues, for the USA, for example, that the country's relative decline in technological leadership is the result of relatively low investment in research and development. Gibson's emphasis on the level of R & D as being the crucial variable in technological change and productivity growth may be exaggerated, however. The level of R & D spending does not necessarily reflect the proportion of *successful* innovation. Nor does it capture the significance of each innovation for the economy. For example, R & D spending on teflon coatings has not been as economically significant as R & D spending on the internal combustion engine.

On this point Abernathy and Townsend (1975) suggest that technological inputs have had the least contribution where they are needed most — in mature and stagnant industries. Salomon (1980) argues also that changes in productivity result not so much from the innovations created by R & D spending, but from their diffusion. Consistent with this, Nelson and Winter (1977) suggest that, for an innovation to have a large productivity impact, an innovative user is needed as well as an innovative producer (e.g., USA's Eastern Airlines's introduction of Boeing's first commercial passenger jet). It is for this reason that Piekarz (1983) questions whether it was the fall in the real value of R & D spending, or a slowdown in the rate of diffusion of innovations, that caused the slowdown in productivity advance in the USA in the 1970s. Social factors and market structures that affect the rate of adoption and diffusion of innovations are clearly important in determining the impact of R & D spending on the speed of productivity advance in the economy.

Experience in the USA (Terleckyj, 1980) indicates a stronger relationship between private R & D spending and productivity advance, than between government R & D spending and productivity growth, suggesting that innovations produced under market constraints are likely to diffuse faster than innovations produced in a bureaucratic environment. Scherer (1983) finds that there is a positive association between R & D and the degree of 'concentration' (i.e. dominance by a few firms) in each industry. A large market share enables a firm to appropriate for itself much of the economic advantage of innovations flowing from R & D expenditure; however, while the relationship is positive, it is less than proportional, meaning that, beyond some point, additional market share for a firm has little effect on R & D spending. This is consistent with Myers' (1983) evidence that very large corporations are not contributing their 'fair share' to innovations. Sahal (1983) complicates matters further by noting that while several innovative industries are highly concentrated (oligopolistic), not all oligopolistic (concentrated) industries tend to be innovative. This he explains by suggesting that the technological progressiveness of an industry depends primarily on its *technological base* rather than on its *market structure*. Mansfield (1968) takes the wheel full circle by finding that R & D is actually *inhibited* by increasing firm size, but this result may be explained by Sahal's theory — the large firms in Mansfield's sample have a weaker technological base than the small firms.

The uncertainty of payoffs arising from R & D may also limit spending on it. As Nelson and Winter point out, R & D is an *uncertain* venture. The odds of success are unknown. The level of R & D and the rate of technological progress depend heavily on the degree of optimism among businessmen and their spirit of entrepreneurial aggression, therefore — i.e., on social, not technological factors.

In summary, the contribution of R & D spending to productivity growth is far from being completely understood: it depends on the success of the research and of subsequent innovations in the market place, on the significance of the innovations, on the significance of the sector of the economy where innovation occurs, and on the rate of diffusion of innovations. The correlation between R & D spending and any resultant rate of productivity growth may indeed be tenuous.

It is not possible to analyse the rate of technological advance purely by looking at R & D inputs, therefore, because the relationship between these inputs and technological change outputs varies according to the environment in which the innovative process is taking place. On the other hand, inventive and innovative *output* is very difficult to measure. Some authors (e.g., Jewkes et al., 1969; Mansfield, 1968) have analysed small samples of specific inventions and innovations. However, to obtain aggregate measures of the rate of technological output is a much more difficult exercise. Most writers looking for measures of technological output have used the rate of patenting activity as the measure. A *patent* is a certificate of ownership which confers a monopoly right for a limited period for a given piece of intellectual property with an industrial application (Bosworth, 1983a).

There are many problems associated with using the number of patents as a measure of technological advance. Patents differ in quality; there are international differences in what is patentable; patent laws change over time; and not all technological inventions or innovations are patented (Stoneman, 1983). Despite these reservations, however, following the path-breaking work of Schmookler (1966), analysis of patents has formed an important part of research into technological change.

Determinants of the rate of technological change

Based on the measures of technological change just outlined we can now go on to consider the determinants of such change. Some of this discussion has already been alluded to in passing. First, how can we explain the level of expenditure on R & D? Stoneman (1983) has summarized the predictions of theoretical economics concerning R & D spending with special reference to R & D per unit of sales (which has been a widely used measure of a firm's 'dynamic efficiency'). At the level of the firm, he argues, economic theory suggests the following: that R & D expenditure as a proportion of the firm's sales will be positively correlated with the effectiveness of R & D in reducing costs, and negatively correlated with market share (i.e., that the greater is the *expected response of rivals* to output change or technology change, the lower will be firms' R & D-to-sales ratio — a result which may provide a link between R & D spending and market structure); that early innovation will be associated with greater *future* expected returns and lower *current* profitability; and that the optimum degree of rivalry for early innovation with major expected returns involves a market structure intermediate between monopoly and large numbers of competitors. Markets with large numbers of competitors favour early introduction only for innovations with modest expected returns.

Empirical studies have concentrated on the influence of firm size and industry concentration on R & D activity. Kamien and

Schwartz (1975) have undertaken a good review of these studies. As mentioned earlier, they find that (with the notable exception of the chemical industry) R & D activity appears to increase with firm size up to a point, then level off or decline beyond it; and that little support has been found for the hypothesis that R & D activity increases monopoly power. A market structure intermediate between monopoly and perfect competition would appear to promote the highest rate of R & D activity (Kamien and Schwartz, 1975, p. 32).

Of course it is precisely in these sorts of 'rivalrous' market structures that aggressive entrepreneurship flourishes (see Chapter 4). High levels of R & D activity may be an expression of entrepreneurial vigour rather than market concentration *per se*.

The next question is what influences the rate of patenting activity? The so-called 'Schmooklerian hypothesis' (based on analysis of patenting activity — see Schmookler, 1966) is that technological progress is 'demand led', i.e. that patented inventions tend to be distributed among industries in proportion to the distribution of investment in plant and equipment. Stoneman (1983) points out that the hypothesis has not met with wholehearted research support, however. And empirical research done by Stoneman and others (Rosenberg, 1974; Scherer, 1982) has shown that the cost of producing *inventions* is also important. According to Stoneman, it is necessary to modify Schmookler's view to one in which both demand and technological opportunity determine the level of patenting activity.

The evidence on firm size, market power and patenting activity is also mixed. The beneficial effect on patenting activity of 'bigness and fewness' is unclear, just as the beneficial effect of 'bigness and fewness' on R & D activity is not entirely clear (see Mansfield, 1968; Bosworth and Wilson, 1980; Stoneman, 1983). Jewkes et al. (1969) looked at sixty-four major twentieth-century inventions. Of these they found that forty could be attributed to individual inventors and twenty-four to corporate R & D. In another sample of twenty-seven inventions, Hamberg (1966) found that only seven came from the R & D units of firms. A study in the aluminium industry (Peek, 1962) found that only seventeen out of 149 major inventions came from major firms.

Looking at *innovations*, however, we find a rather different story. For example, Jewkes et al. found that of the forty 'external' inventions, at least half needed a major corporate R & D effort in development before innovation occurred. This takes us back again to the question of firm size and innovation. To quote Freeman (1982, p. 137):

> The relative performance of large firms is apparently better with respect to innovations than with respect to inventions, and Jewkes accepts that their role in *development* work (which is usually far more expensive) is much more important.

Mansfield (1968) has undertaken statistical analysis of innovation and firm size which suggests that large firms account for more than their market share of innovations, though this did not apply in all industries. The advantage of large firms was particularly apparent for innovations which had high investment requirements, and where the largest four firms were particularly large compared with other firms. Mansfield also found that the rate of *process* innovation varied substantially over the business cycle but that rate of *product* innovation did not vary significantly over the business cycle.

Freeman (1982) reports survey evidence from two surveys relating the number of innovations to firm size. Table 2 brings together evidence from these two surveys.

Freeman suggests that 'on the reasonable assumption that the branches of industry included in the survey are representative of

Table 2   Percentage of innovations according to firm size, 1945-1980

Number of employees	1945-9 %	1950-4 %	1955-9 %	1960-4 %	1965-9 %	1970-4 %	1975-80 %	Total %
1-199	16.0	12.0	11.0	11.0	13.0	15.0	17.0	14.0
						(11.0)	(12.0)	(12.0)
200-499	9.0	6.0	8.0	6.0	7.0	9.0	7.0	7.0
						(7.0)	(6.0)	(7.0)
500-999	3.0	2.0	7.0	5.0	5.0	4.0	3.0	4.0
						(4.0)	(3.0)	(4.0)
1000-9999	36.0	36.0	25.0	27.0	23.0	17.0	14.0	23.0
						(19.0)	(13.0)	(23.0)
10 000 and over	36.0	44.0	50.0	51.0	52.0	55.0	59.0	52.0
						(59.0)	(66.0)	(54.0)
TOTAL	100.0	100.0	100.0	100.0	100.0	100.0	100.0	100.0
No. of innovations	94	191	274	405	467	401	461	2293

(Note: numbers in parentheses for the periods 1970-74 and 1975-80 are the weighted percentage contributions, assuming the same sectoral mix as in the period 1945-69.)

Source: Freeman (1971); Townsend et al. (1982)

British industry as a whole', the most important conclusions were these:

1   Small firms accounted for about 12 per cent of all industrial innovations made since the war. This may be compared with their share of production and employment, which in 1963 amounted to about 19 per cent of net output and 22 per cent of employment.
2   The share of small firms in innovation has apparently been fairly steady, but their share of output and employment has been falling.
3   The share of the largest firms (10 000 employees and over) in the total number of innovations increased substantially over the period, at the expense of medium-sized firms (1000–9999 employees).

Analysis by branch of industry showed big variations in the contribution of small firms to innovation. Industries could be classified into two groups:

a   Those in which small enterprises made little or no discernible contribution to innovation, either absolutely or relatively. These included aerospace, motor vehicles, dyes, pharmaceuticals, cement, glass, steel, aluminium, synthetic resins and shipbuilding and (in a special category) coal and gas. In this group, small firms accounted for only just over 1 per cent of innovations (six out of a total of 479), but about 8 per cent of net output in 1963.
b   Those in which small enterprises made a fairly significant contribution to innovation in the industry concerned. These included scientific instruments, electronics, carpets, textiles, textile machinery, paper and board, leather and footwear, timber and furniture, and construction. In this group small enterprises accounted for 103 out of 523 innovations, or about 17 per cent, compared with about 20 per cent of net output in 1963.

Freeman suggests that probably the greatest advantage of the small firm lies in flexibility, concentration and internal communications. Shimonshi (1970), who studied the electronic scientific instrument industry, also found that new, small firms had played a critical part in innovating several key instruments and postulated that other main advantages lay in motivation, low costs, short lead-time on development work (because of speed in making decisions), and flexibility. He assigned numerical values to these advantages (see Table 3).

Table 3 Comparative advantage of types of firms in instrument innovation

Innovation process	Established large firm	Recently-established small firm producing second or subsequent products	Entrepreneur, first product
Motivation to innovate	3	1–	1
Ability to have or develop own knowledge, technology	1	3	1
Cost advantages, using outside knowledge	2	3	1
Resources available to penetrate market	1	2–	3
Resources for new product development	1	3	1 or 2
Advantage in costs and speed of prototype and early model manufacture	3	1–	1
Flexibility to adopt new product or technology	3	2	1+
Cost advantage, large series production and marketing	1	2–	3

1 = highest comparative advantages, 3 = lowest comparative advantages

Source: Shimonshi (1970, p. 61)

A major research project — project SAPPHO — carried out during the 1970s by the Science Policy Research Unit at Sussex University represents probably the most thorough and detailed attempt to test hypotheses about the sources of successful innovation (see Freeman, 1982). The first stage was a study of fifty-eight attempted innovations in chemicals and scientific instruments. At a later stage additional innovations were studied in the same industries, plus some innovations in the mechanical engineering industry.

Project SAPPHO suggested that success is associated with:

1 strong in-house professional R&D;
2 careful attention to the potential market and substantial efforts to involve, educate, and assist users;
3 entrepreneurship that is strong enough to co-ordinate R&D, production and marketing effectively;
4 good communications with the outside scientific world and customers; and

5   the use of patents to gain protection and to bargain with
    customers.

This list of attributes, and those of the successful small innovating
firms cited earlier by Freeman and Shimonshi, read remarkably like'
the attributes of Peters and Waterman's 'excellent' firms in *In Search
of Excellence* (1983).

As we have already noted, invention and innovation do not have
a great impact on the economy until the use of that technology is
widespread. But why, if a new technology is superior, is it not taken
up immediately by all potential users? Numerous empirical studies
have found that the *diffusion* path is typically 'S-shaped'. In the case
of inter-firm diffusion, consider N_t as the number of firms using new
technology in time (t) in a fixed population of firms, P. If we plot
N_t/P against time (t) we find an S-shaped curve as in Figure 3. The
upper limit of the curve has a maximum of 1.

Theoretical approaches to *intra-firm* diffusion include the Mansfield 'epidemic approach' (Mansfield, 1968) and 'Bayesian learning'

Figure 3 **The 'S-shaped' diffusion curve**

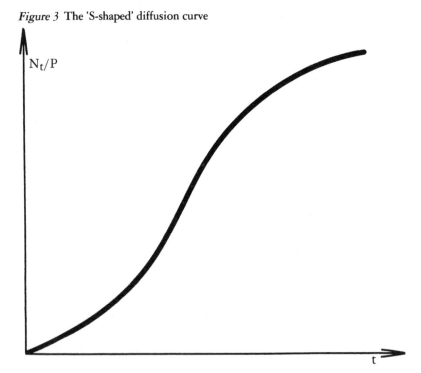

N_t/P

t

models (Stoneman, 1981; Lindner, Fischer and Pardey, 1979). Both approaches accord reductions in uncertainty a major role in the determination of the diffusion path. Empirical studies of *inter-firm* diffusion, however, do not provide very definite conclusions. Stoneman (1983) discusses *intra-sectoral* diffusion. He concludes (p. 110) that:

> ... the empirical work ... suggests that profitability has a major role to play in the determination of diffusion speed, as do absolute capital requirements. The role played by market structure is somewhat ambiguous, but there seems to be some indication that larger firms are earlier adopters ...

When looking at *economy-wide* diffusion, different theoretical approaches have again been taken — for example the 'Schumpeter approach', the 'vintage approach' and the 'stock adjustment approach'. Schumpeter's hypothesis (Schumpeter, 1934) was that new inventions are made when the economy is in the trough of the cycle. The first application of these inventions is by an entrepreneur who makes temporary excess profit from his path-breaking activities. This leads to imitation from other economic actors ('Austrian' entrepreneurs) (see Reekie, 1979). So diffusion proceeds and leads to changes in factor and product prices which tend to force non-adopters to use the new technology. Gross investment is boosted by the take-up of new technology which produces an upswing in the cycle with a multiplier effect. As the diffusion process slows down, the strength of the boom dies away and the process goes into reverse. This approach has not been used for empirical analysis. 'Vintage' models take technical progress to be completely 'embodied' in new capital stock; therefore, its economy-wide diffusion depends on the rate of investment. Salter developed this approach to diffusion in some detail (Salter, 1966).

Nasbeth and Ray (1974) produce some interesting empirical results on economy-wide diffusion. Table 4 reproduces their results on the factors influencing the diffusion of numerically-controlled machine tools in different countries. In this table,

> the ten probably most essential factors are listed to explain differences in actual diffusion in the various countries. These factors were selected in accordance with the findings of the inquiry ... Using a scale ranging from +5 to –5, each factor was

given a 'valuation', which when multiplied by the weight gave a score for each factor. (Nasbeth and Ray, 1974, p. 57)

Of particular note is the importance accorded to high wage levels in determining diffusion speeds. The explanation is probably that high wages imply a high return to the introduction of numerically-controlled machine tools. This appears to reflect the importance of profitability as a cause of diffusion speed.

The literature on the *international* diffusion of innovation — i.e., on cross-cultural technology transfer — demonstrates that although licensing arrangements can be used, direct investment is the most important institutional arrangement by which technology is transferred. This takes the analysis directly to consideration of multi-national companies. Direct investment is thought to follow (risk-adjusted) profitability considerations.

Productivity growth and technological change

In an excellent review of research on productivity growth and productivity differences, Nelson (1981) reasserts the limitations of the conventional (so-called 'neo-classical') economic approach in explaining productivity growth. He states that 'virtually all scholars of productivity growth rates agree on the central role of technological advance', and, further, emphasizes the importance of R & D spending in this process, but notes the inadequacy of the conventional economic approach in explaining the relation between research and development and technological advance. In addition, he argues that getting away from the conventional strait-jacket allows research on technological change and productivity growth to benefit from a greater breadth of understanding on two other fronts:

> The first is the nature of the variables affecting productivity at the level of the individual firm, and the sources of differences in productivity among firms. As suggested, there is a substantial body of literature which does not see a firm simply as a profit seeking 'chooser' of inputs and technology operating within a framework of widely available technological knowledge, and known factor prices. Rather, it sees a firm as a 'social system', which motivates its members in greater or lesser degree, and which influences how managerial decisions are carried out and how alternatives are perceived and evaluated. Several studies of inter-firm productivity differences have found social systems related variables, as well as neo-classical ones, to be important.

Table 4 Factors affecting the diffusion of numerically controlled machines

	Weight	Austria		Italy		Sweden		UK		USA		West Germany	
		Value	Score	Value	Score	Value	Score	Value	Score	Value	Score	Value	Score
Wage level	40	+1	40	—	—	+3	120	+2	80	+5	200	+2	80
Importance of aerospace industry	10	—	—	+1	10	+1	10	+4	40	+5	50	+1	10
Quality of information system	10	+2	20	—	—	+4	40	+4	40	+5	50	+2	20
Investment financing possibilities	10	—	—	—	—	+4	40	+3	30	+5	50	+1	10
Management attitudes	5	—	—	—	—	+3	15	+2	10	+5	25	+1	5
Condition of the market	5	+1	5	+1	5	+3	15	+4	20	+3	15	+5	25
Trade union attitudes	5	—	—	—	—	—	—	-2	-10	-4	-20	+1	5
Technical factors	5	—	—	+1	5	+2	10	+3	15	+5	25	+1	5
Labour market conditions	5	—	—	+1	5	+5	25	+2	10	—	—	+4	20
Other relevant factors	5	+2	10	+3	15	+3	15	+5	25	+5	25	+5	25
Total	100		75		40		290		260		420		205

Source: Nasbeth and Ray (1974), p. 56

In addition, these studies document significant differences in technologies employed by different firms, differences not readily explained on neo-classical grounds ... [The other] is the connections among and the factors behind the proximate sources of growth treated in growth accounting. It is apparent that these sources interact strongly. Capital accumulation and education support technological progress. At the same time, the returns to physical investment and increased education depend on technological progress. This suggests that in deepening the analysis of growth we ought to consider not only forces that affect the proximate sources singularly, but also more general features of the economic environment, and all political and social institutions that support all three sources and the growth they promote. We are, therefore, led to a concern with international differences and intertemporal changes in the economic environment and institutions. (Nelson, 1981, p. 1036)

On the firm as a social system Nelson goes on to say that:

Given the perhaps considerable range of flexibility left by technology and managerial instructions and overview, the social system of work sets norms, enforces them, and resists pressures or commands from management that are inconsistent with those norms. The lower levels of representatives of management, such as foremen whose function is to monitor and discipline performance, are at least partially co-opted into the social system. Consistent with classical organisation theory, certain ways of doing things and certain performance levels will be established and adhered to, but contrary to the reasoning of classical theory, these will be influenced as much by the social system as by the management's directions and pressures. On the other hand, these procedures and norms can be influenced by the sentiments and attitudes of the workers, and by the tone of the organisation more generally. Management may have a good deal to do with what that tone is. How workers feel about their job, about their fellow workers, about management, and about the organisation, may be more important in influencing productivity than is the particular way they are instructed to do their work, the formal organisational structure, or even financial incentives. (Nelson, 1981, p. 1038)

This important aspect of the analysis of productivity growth is confronted in detail in Chapter 5.

Nelson goes on to discuss whether regulation and the growth of the welfare state have inhibited technological change and productivity growth:

> The greatly enlarged regimes of regulation and the growth of the welfare state also have been identified with developments strongly influencing productivity growth. While some analyses of the effects of these new institutions have focused strictly on their resource absorbing or diverting aspects, other scholars have recognised that their effects are atmospheric, like the microeconomic climate, the state of labor relations, and the character of a society's educational system. Businessmen, discussing their concerns about the regulatory environment, stress the uncertainties involved and their fears that anything they try to do that is new will be prohibited. This fear influences decision making regarding R & D and physical investment. Similarly, it has been argued that the most pernicious effect of the rise of the welfare state is that some young people no longer feel that they should or must work very hard for a living. No persuasive evidence as yet supports any of these contentions. I mention them only to call attention to the fact that they have no place in orthodox analysis. (Nelson, 1981, p. 1057)

Eads (1980) also looks at regulation and concludes somewhat differently, however (p. 54):

> Regulation is indeed likely to change both the level and direction of innovative activity ... But our knowledge both of regulation and of the innovation process is too primitive for us to tell precisely what these changes will be. Rather than make major changes in the regulatory process on the grounds that they will aid innovation, we are better advised to confine our attention to improving the general climate for innovation and altering those aspects of regulation that even casual investigation may suggest be deleterious. That, by and large, is the direction suggested by most recent important studies; their degree of caution is appropriate.

Hitherto, little attention has been paid in this chapter to the relationship between technological change and the labour force, though we have indicated the virtue of considering the firm as a social system and thereby incorporating work organization and worker attitudes in the analysis.

First let us consider the influence of labour force characteristics on the process of technological change. Technological change can be embodied in the labour force as well as the capital stock. Hence, policy planners are concerned about the skill mix of the labour force and the amount of qualified manpower. Caution must be expressed here, however, against the conclusion that technological change can be induced by increasing school retention rates or participation in further or higher education. Nelson (1981, p. 1055), makes the point very well:

> Just as a high rate of capital formation and a well educated work force stimulate and facilitate technological advance, so technological advance stimulates a high rate of capital formation and motivates young people to acquire formal education. If technological advance were slower, diminishing returns to capital deepening would have less of an offset, and the returns to investment or the investment rate or both would be lower. If technological advance were slower, there would be less demand for scientists and engineers to enable firms to stay competitive with their technological rivals. There would be less need for managers and workers to deal with new situations and to learn new skills.
>
> From this perspective, it would be surprising if one observed many countries where technological advance was rapid, but where investment rates and educational attainments were low. Nor would one expect to find many instances where capital formation maintained a rapid rate, but new technologies were not being introduced and spread through the economy. Societies might find it hard to sustain high educational attainments on the part of young people entering the work force, and not at the same time be moderately progressive scientifically and technologically. In short, there are not neatly separable sources of growth, but rather a package of elements all of which need to be there.

That is not to say that the manpower requirements of technological progress are not important, but these are likely to be induced by the demands of technologically progressive firms. It might be added, however, that on-the-job training as well as formal education are important in the process and that the type and quality of training and education deserve attention as much, if not more, than the quantity of qualified manpower.

On the impact of technological progress on the labour force, there are various issues. Concern is often expressed that the productivity improvement associated with technological progress, especially when combined with labour-saving technological change, is likely to cause unemployment. Historical evidence from the experience of mechanization and automation tends to contradict this. (There is also the question of 'de-skilling' resulting from technological change: this issue is dealt with at length in Chapter 5.)

Australian research

As was noted earlier, Australian economic analysis of technological change is somewhat limited, but some researchers have done useful work. For example, Peter Stubbs undertook an important project in the 1960s and it was published as *Innovation and Research: A Study in Australian Industry* (Stubbs, 1968a). This included a comparison of Australian R & D efforts with other industrialized countries, and of Australian patenting activity. Amongst his conclusions were that 'the distribution of research effort in Australia is weighted in favour of research and against development'. Analysis of patenting did not provide a very encouraging picture of Australian technological progress, either. Stubbs also reported the results of a survey of forty-five manufacturing companies, which gave additional extensive information about their R & D and innovation. The survey showed a high level of dependence on overseas technology, though it suggested that industry conducted more R & D than had been generally realized. Commercial success, however, rested upon a much wider variety of factors than expenditure on R & D.

In a more recent book, *Technology and Australia's Future* (1980), Stubbs updated some of this evidence. The following extract (pp. 22–3) is of special relevance:

> One of the casualties of the 1970s has been technical innovation. Across much of the decade industrial R & D in real terms in Britain and Australia actually declined, while in the United States in the latter 1970s it was more or less static. There were also changes of emphasis within research budgets, especially in the United States. There the growing emphasis on environmental issues, often concerned to rectify the social costs of technology, put severe constraints on innovation in such industries as pharmaceuticals (OECD, 1979) and automobiles ... Basic research was hard pressed because it is more risky and slow to pay off, since it has to be subject to applied work and development before it reaches the market: the emphasis shifted more towards low risk development work with a relatively quick pay-back.

It has been suggested (OECD, 1979) that this reduction of R & D expenditure and the increased need to concentrate on energy and environmental issues has serious implications for the rate of economic growth in advanced economies. If that is the case, then Australia has grounds for serious disquiet. The following newly released figures for R & D expenditure [see Table 5, below] reveal that despite a small increase in R & D expenditure by business enterprise, it is still far below the real level of 1973/74.

Table 5   R & D expenditure in Australian business enterprises

		1973/74	1976/77	1978/79
(a)	*At current prices ($M)*			
	Private sector	190.4	160.4	204.5
	Public sector businesses	na	42.4	39.1
	Total business enterprise	na	202.8	243.6
(b)	*At constant 1973/74 prices*			
	Private sector	236.3	124.1	132.1
	Public sector businesses	na	33.0	26.2
	Total business enterprise	na	157.1	158.3

Source: Stubbs (1980), p. 23

Another useful discussion of R & D in Australia was submitted by Gannicott to the Committee of Inquiry into Technological Change in Australia (Gannicott, 1980). In the same collection, there are two papers, one by Kasper and one by Lydall on 'Technological Change and Economic Growth' (Kasper, 1980; Lydall, 1980). Updating earlier work by Robertson (1978), Kasper states that

> the conclusion ... that technology and allied forces added relatively little to rising living standards (in Australia) — does not vary much if we extend the period of observation: for 1950–51 to 1973–74 the 'third factor' share is 33%, for 1950–51 to 1978–79 it is also 33% (Kasper, 1980, p. 251).

Kasper goes on, however, to make very optimistic observations about the future potential of technological change in Australia (pp. 255–6):

> The opportunities for Australians to reap very major benefits from technological and other structural changes seem, in the next decades, considerably better than for most Northern Hemisphere industrial countries. Australia has an endowment with land, energy, skills, labour, political-social infrastructure, capital

and basic technology that is not equalled by many other affluent societies, and Australia is the only major industrial society with a European life style near the world's industrially most dynamic region, eastern Asia (including China). This has changed the 'tyranny of distance' into a potential for fast growth.

A recently conducted survey of future probable innovations (reported in Kasper et al., 1980, pp. 155–67 and 229–31) has shown that one can identify several complexes of technological change which could reinforce existent Australian comparative industrial advantages considerably, if Australians are quick to innovate and quick to adjust over the next two decades:

- energy substitution (especially coal technology)
- specialised micro-electronics
- biotechnology (in agriculture and medicine)
- materials substitution

These complexes of technical innovation (and many new technologies in other areas) are likely to open many market opportunities to enterprising firms. But it will of course be critical whether the socio-economic system encourages constructive responses or not. The responses of the economic system to those technological challenges (and the benefits of income and employment growth to Australians) will depend critically on whether this country continues to follow an interventionist and protectionist path of economic policy or whether Australia liberalises, opens up and faces the risks and opportunities of trying out new solutions to solve new problems.

Stubbs (1980) also refers to the importance of social attitudes in the capacity of societies to take effective advantage of technological potentials. In particular he points out (pp. 122–3):

There is often an unwholesome contrast in attitudes to new technology, epitomised by microprocessors, in Australia and Britain on the one hand, and the United States, West Germany and Japan on the other. Where the latter view and espouse new technology with alacrity, as a means to increased efficiency and competitiveness, powerful elements in the former emphasise the drawbacks. These conservative elements fail to realise that it is not enough to say that some people may lose (albeit temporarily) from new technology; it is more to the point to say that even more people would lose even greater amounts if the technology is ignored or baulked. The problems of granting some form of accommodation to losers are real enough, but the likelihood of doing so is measurably greater in a vigorous, innovative growing economy than in one which is hobbled by reactionary conservatism of whatever political complexion.

Finally, let us consider work by Metcalfe and Hall (1983) and Kaspura and Ho-Trieu (1980). Metcalf and Hall investigate the 'Verdoorn Law' with Australian data. The results confirm the relevance of the Verdoorn Law to Australian manufacturing experience: i.e. industries with above-average rates of output growth experience above-average rates of productivity growth. They go on to analyse the employment implications. 'It would appear ... that the direct labour displacing effects of productivity growth are more than offset by indirect compensating mechanisms which increase the rate of growth of output significantly to expand employment' (Metcalf and Hall, 1983, pp. 366–7). They go on to explain this in terms of the 'Salter Mechanism', whereby increases in productivity lead to reductions in price and increases in product demand. Empirical support is provided.

Kaspura and Ho-Trieu (1980) use a conventional economic framework to come to very similar conclusions (pp. 20–1):

> While labour input declined in the majority of industries we were unable to find a general relationship between growth in labour input and technological change. However, technological change was positively correlated with output growth. Similarly, there was a positive correlation between output growth and labour input growth suggesting that the decline in manufacturing employment is associated with low or negative output growth in many industries. We showed that production costs and relative prices were negatively correlated with technological change. In other words, poor growth in total input productivity, or technological change, has meant that many industries have been unable to contain production costs, and so maintain competitive relative prices. Taken together the evidence suggests that technological change was not the cause of manufacturing unemployment during the study period. However, it would appear that a failure to attain technological advance has been a major cause of the problems experienced by many industries.

Having reviewed existing research on the economics of the process of technological change and its relationship with productivity growth, we believe there are some specific research projects which could be usefully undertaken in Australia in this area. Some of the suggestions that follow imply the use of existing data; for others it would be necessary to generate new data. Some of the suggestions involve research which is reasonably self-contained, but the emphasis is on moving towards an eclectic approach and considering a wide range of influences on productivity growth.

First, it would be useful to bring together existing data on technology in Australia from primary and secondary sources. Then the potential use of these data can be reviewed and gaps highlighted.

Second, we recommend an analysis of research and development in Australia, enlarging on the previous work in this area (Stubbs, 1968, 1980; Gannicott, 1980) and investigating the links between R & D and productivity growth.

Third, we suggest further investigation into the potential analysis of inventions and innovative activity using patent data.

Fourth, diffusion of innovations in Australia is a particularly important area for research. As noted earlier, invention and innovation do not have a great impact on the economy until the use or ownership of that technology is widespread. The rate of diffusion of, say, microprocessors in Australia should be investigated and compared, if possible, with their diffusion in other countries. Another promising way to investigate the 'specialness' of Australia with respect to the diffusion process, is to investigate the behaviour of multinationals in Australia. Do they adopt new technology in Australia slower or faster than in other countries, and why?

Fifth, a project SAPPHO (see p. 33), studying attempted innovations in certain key industries should be undertaken. Given the international importance of project SAPPHO in the evidence about successful innovations, a comparable project in Australia, aimed at highlighting similar causes and influences with special reference to the Australian socio-economic system, could prove very useful.

Sixth, we need a study of productivity improvement, using a multidisciplinary approach. Project SAPPHO focused on comparing successful and unsuccessful innovations. An alternative approach, placing innovation in a broader context would be to focus on productivity growth as the central feature to explain. A sample of firms, perhaps from two different industries, could be analysed with respect to their rate of change of productivity.

Seventh, the relationship between static and dynamic efficiency should be investigated. We have argued strongly that economic success should be analysed in a dynamic context. It would be interesting to know if attempts to obtain static gains from economies of scale diminish the probability of dynamic gains from innovation. Another area for analysis is the link between the rate of new investment, the age of capital, and capital utilization.

Eighth, further research is necessary to investigate how the short-run macro-economic constraints on economic growth might be overcome to allow the economy to return to a path of low inflation, low unemployment and high productivity growth.

Ninth, the manpower requirements of technologically progressive firms, and factors contributing to labour mobility, are issues worthy of research. On the employment implications of technological change, we favour the case study approach (it could possibly be incorporated in the sixth project, outlined above).

4 The Effects of Market Structures on Competitiveness

It may be true that necessity is the 'mother of invention', but the steady pressure of competition is the mother of innovation, i.e. of practical applications that raise productivity. When we speak of competition here, we refer to a dynamic process of *economic rivalry* between various suppliers of the same product or reasonably close substitutes. Such rivalry is motivated by the effort of firms to obtain and retain a profit through a dynamic process in which each supplier tries to secure a 'market niche' (Lindbeck, 1981) — i.e. tries to reach a state in which competitive pressures are reduced — or tries to expand its already-existing niche. For example, radio stations frequently aim at particular sections of the potential listener audience; a type of car or a style of clothes is often aimed at a particular group of potential car or clothing customers. Rivalry between suppliers is a persistent sequence of defensive and aggressive actions. Each supplier faces a demand for his product or service as depicted in Figure 4. Around the price at which he sells is a 'niche' price range within which there would be scope to raise or lower the price without much effect on the quantities sold in that 'niche'. Only when prices are raised or lowered by a considerable percentage will sizeable quantity responses occur.

The reasons why individual suppliers have such a scope for price variations are two. First, nearly every product is slightly different from even its closest rival. Even close substitutes have slight differences in technical properties, so that the buyer of each may not switch in response to small price changes. Second, the costs of gaining knowledge about products, the costs of transport and communication and the benefits of continuing buyer-seller linkages create preferences for particular sellers among some buyers.

Producers will often try to widen their scope for price variation, either by actual product differentiation or by creating notional product differences through advertising. They do this because they operate under conditions of uncertainty and risk. Modern firms have high overhead costs so that fluctuations in the flow of production lead to considerable cost fluctuations. If firms cannot pass on at least some of the increases in costs (when they occur) in the form of higher prices without having to fear massive losses in market shares, they would have to face wildly fluctuating profits and production levels (which would increase the risk of the enterprise). Entrepreneurs and managers try — like all human beings — to avoid unforeseen fluctuations and changes. A market niche with a reasonably wide range of acceptable prices is a degree of insurance in an inevitably changing world.

Figure 4 'Niche' Competition

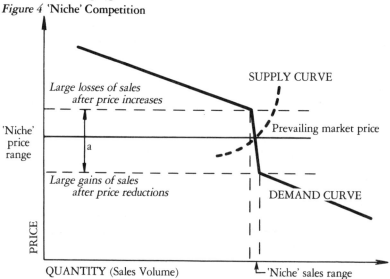

If economic rivalry is lively, competitors will try to erode each other's market niches, either by trying to imitate successful product variations by rivals (i.e., variations that raised a competitor's market share or widened his market niche) or by undercutting his price. *This competitive rivalry — even the latent fear of it — induces producers to search continually for innovation, either productivity-enhancing process innovations that cut costs, or product innovations that secure or widen market niches.*

This type of rivalry is often most pronounced when it takes place among a few sizeable competitors, whereas 'perfectly competitive' industries containing very large numbers of small competitors selling very similar products (such as wheatgrowers, petrol retailers, delicatessens) often operate in a state of 'night cap competition'

(Machlup) which may produce socially less desirable *dynamic* results, i.e. slower productivity advance than rivalry among few competitors for a market.

Rivalry among a few firms *may* produce dynamic change — but there is no guarantee that an active state of rivalry will always exist. It is possible that the rivals will seek to reach a state of peace in which there is much explicit and implicit collusion between them and in which there is no active pressure on each rival's established market niche. Such a state of the market is less risky and more comfortable for producers, but of course — in the longer run — less conducive to economic growth and stable cost and price levels. Peace between rivals tends to prevail where governments inhibit competition by regulation, intervention and protection from small, not-yet-established suppliers (who have much to gain and little to lose from 'having a go'). Because competitive pressure on each firm's market niche is so uncomfortable, established producers often use their lobbying powers to obtain a government umbrella for their niche. Situations of 'natural monopoly' (for example, electricity distribution), where purely technical conditions inhibit genuine and active competition, tend to be much rarer than government-supported suppression of market rivalry. Indeed, monopolies will usually act as though they had competitors if the threat of entry from potential rivals exists. Thus, the sort of market structure which is consistent with rapid productivity advance is what has been described as a 'contestable market'. When the entry of new rivals becomes difficult (for example, because of government protection of established producers), productivity advance slows.

How important are economies of scale?

It is sometimes said that the Australian market is so small and fragmented among the States that the most efficient scale of output cannot be achieved by Australian firms, except perhaps by monopoly enterprises whose protected position will, then, give them no incentive to achieve high productivity performance and advance. If this were true, there would be an insoluble dilemma confronting efforts to increase the rate of productivity among Australian enterprises.

Fortunately, the proposition is untrue on three counts. First, the potential size of market niches is determined by the *world* market, not the domestic Australian market. The alleged inability of Australian firms to achieve full economies of scale (and highest productivity) results from a focus by Australian enterprises on rivalry for the domestic market only. Australian producers could, instead of aiming to fill all domestic market niches from local production at small, low-productivity scales of output, aim to fill some world market niches. Since the world market (measured by GDP) is fifty times the size of the Australian market, the number of Australian enterprises that could reach full economies of scale is theoretically limitless. Second, provided the Australian market remains 'contestable' by foreign rivals, there is no reason to suppose that Australian monopoly enterprises will not strive for maximum productivity and productivity advance to keep potential rivals at bay. Our problems arise from the sheltering by government of Australian monopolies from the threat of new rivals (domestic and overseas), in response to pressures from the capital and labour interests associated with the local producer. Third, economies of scale are not nearly so important as conventional economic theory would lead one to suppose. Beyond a surprisingly small size, as Peters and Waterman (1983) argue, *diseconomies* of scale set in with a vengeance, resulting from the escalating costs of communication, co-ordination and decision-making, the increasing remoteness of management from workforce, and the loss of enthusiasm and sense of purpose by the people 'at the coal-face', i.e. the workers.

The more successful large organizations have overcome this problem by splitting into much smaller autonomous units. The emphasis is on small *teams* of ten or so persons in size. What these enterprises lose in scale economies is more than made up in dynamic economies — innovations, flexibility, and enthusiasm, and hence, fast productivity advance. The advantages of the 'big bet' on large-scale production facilities are only short-term, if they exist at all, as the resulting lumbering industrial dinosaurs are surpassed by newer technologies and newer and better products tailored by their more dynamic, smaller rivals to the ever-changing needs of the market. 'Small is beautiful; small is effective' applies generally in determining the *dynamic* competitiveness of enterprises in an uncertain world (Klein, 1977, pp. 35–67). The importance placed on scale economies derives from emphasis on static economies in a world of certainty. The *static* advantages of bigness are always eventually overtaken by the *dynamic* advantages of smallness. This is increasingly being recognized. For example, Nevis' (1983) examination of the Chinese economy concludes that in that country there is a need to break down its large, cumbersome, low-productivity bureaucracy: loyalty and commitment is easier to attain in small social units than in large units. Myers (1983) cites statistics indicating that large corporations in the USA are not contributing their 'fair share' of innovations — in particular, of product innovations (as opposed to product improvements or process innovations). Swann (1975) argues that in development of some industries, small firms get a start because larger companies have not exploited the opportunities presented. It is testimony to the lack of dynamic perspective of many Australian enterprises that they give so much emphasis to economies of scale as an excuse for not possessing a greater degree of competitiveness. Scale economies do count — but for much less than is popularly supposed. (Research into the static and dynamic economies of scale of industrial production processes would be very useful because it would alert Australian firms to potential productivity gains (and losses) from changes in scale.) In any event, with a world market niche rather than an Australian market niche in view, the problems of being unable to reach sufficient scale economies simply evaporate.

What also matters frequently is not an aggregated market for a set of related products. In modern industry, scale economies can often be reaped in small, individual production processes of small component parts, if transport and communications with partner countries are cheap and efficient. (The productivity-raising role of cost-efficient transport and communication within Australia and with our overseas trade partners might be another extremely useful area of productivity research.) The relevant market for Australians to consider is often not, say, the market for passenger vehicles, but the markets for engine blocks, panels or gearboxes — items in which Australia could specialize, reaping large productivity gains through mass production of various component lines.

This kind of enterprise depends, of course, on reasonably free international trade. There are other benefits too. International trade liberalization promotes the international transmission of constructive ideas, stimulates competitive rivalry and productivity increases. As already noted, these dynamic gains from trade are more important in most industrial markets than the allocative gains touted in the usual textbook models, which normally assume productivity growth away. Trade liberalization would allow the Australian suppliers to specialize in whatever products or processes they had international comparative advantage. (What precisely our comparative advantages are have to be *discovered*, by that most sophisticated discovery procedure, market competition.) Australia's most enterprising, imaginative producers are those with most to gain, but it is likely that there would also be relatively few absolute losers, since such a stimulus would accelerate overall growth in productivity, incomes and demand. As Klein (1977, p. 43) points out, 'dynamic efficiency games are non-zero sum', i.e., everyone can gain. The experience of the industrial countries of Europe in the 1950s and 1960s — when they went through such a process of competitive market integration and dynamic productivity growth — shows that this experience is socially exhilarating. And the successful experiences of many Australians in the more competitive markets of Hong Kong and California shows that Australians, too, can prosper greatly under genuine competition.

A useful project for research into productivity advance in Australia would be to document the experiences of such Australian firms that have moved successfully into more competitive markets overseas, be it by becoming small multinationals or by establishing themselves as exporters. Much could be gained for our understanding of productivity growth if the lessons they learnt (and the conditions for their success) could be isolated and made known more widely to Australians generally.

The standard economics model of the firm, with its focus on equilibrium, misses essential aspects of the economic environment. The *genuine* life of an enterprise, we would argue, is disequilibrium, due to changing expectations and aspirations, uncertainties and risks, exploration of the untested and the unknown. Disequilibrium makes economic endeavour into a never-ending process, in which profit is the reward for risk-taking and for finding new socially desired solutions to economic problems. In such circumstances, profit is a reward that is morally deserved.

Entrepreneurship

A firm can be regarded as a decision-making unit between markets for inputs (labour, capital equipment, materials and semi-finished products) and markets for outputs (products), in a milieu full of rivalry and uncertainty about the future. An *entrepreneur* plays a key role in each firm, because he organizes the combination of inputs and takes the considerable technical and commercial risks of doing so. A genuine entrepreneur (in contrast to a mere manager, who administers production within well-known channels) frequently does not have an established market, but creates one for the new products he plans to supply. The creation of a market for one's product requires not only the development of that product at a price at which there is sufficient demand, but also information-spreading through advertising. In this sense, it is true to say that — with genuine entrepreneurs — supply creates its own demand.

The entrepreneur also has to develop and test production processes and products and — often — to organize the supply of the required inputs, e.g. by training workers. All this is highly risky, both technically and commercially. Whilst some entrepreneurs may enjoy risk-taking in its own right, or may take risks for non-economic reasons (like prestige or the award of an honour), most people do not like to take on major risks without the prospect of material reward. This is the social role of profit. Firms which do not take risks in the course of earning profits might as well be nationalized and run by a risk-averse government bureaucracy.

Entrepreneurial functions go beyond the mainly economic roles discussed so far. In reality, productivity increases require a number of entrepreneurial and managerial functions which transcend the usual narrow definitions in the literature of what makes an entrepreneur. Below is a comprehensive list of functions.

A   Exchange relationships:
   1   perceiving (novel or imitative) market opportunities;
   2   gaining control over scarce resources (or creating critical inputs);
   3   purchasing inputs;
   4   selling the product and responding to competitors.
B   'Political' administration:
   5   dealing with the public bureaucracy (getting permits and licences, taxation);
   6   managing human relations within the firm;
   7   managing human relations with suppliers and customers.
C   Control functions:
   8   controlling finances;
   9   maintaining, and possibly expanding the rate of production.
D   Technical management:
   10 establishing the plant;
   11 supervising industrial engineering including quality control;
   12 promoting innovation of processes and products.

Economists normally stress the aspects in group A, sociologists and behaviouralists focus on group B, management training often focuses on group C, and engineers tend to concentrate on group D. But the functions of the genuine entrepreneur ideally encompass all these twelve areas of endeavour, because they are all important to productivity levels. In complex operations, these various groups of entrepreneurial functions are usually best handled by a team in which the various members complement each other. Work within a trusted team is essential to productivity growth. Excessive individualism, refusal to delegate and lack of team-work can often set limits to productivity growth. Inter-cultural studies have shown that individualist Latin American entrepreneurs, for example, fail to develop industrial productivity to adequate levels, whilst neo-Confucian (East Asian) societies, that are based on team structures needed for rice growing, tend to achieve adequate productivity levels in complex industrial ventures fairly easily, because they rely on, and trust, team structures (Hagen, 1962; Hirschmeier, 1964; Yamamura, 1968).

In fact, this point cannot be overstressed. A major factor distinguishing dynamically competitive and high-productivity enterprises from the rest is their *willingness to decentralize the entrepreneurial function* right down to the factory floor. Workers in these enterprises know that they really count in carving out the present and future competitive place of the enterprise. The task of top management is to establish and maintain values and purpose (what the enterprise is supposed to be about, and not just making money), and 'to get the herd heading roughly West' (Peters and Waterman, 1983, p. 115). After that, it is the people 'at the coal face' who count, not the management. Management's job is to inspire the workers, to help the workers get the job done. This form of organization can be regarded as functioning 'bottom-up' rather than 'top-down' as the usual structure of 'control' implies. It is the antithesis of grand planning from the top; it is evolution from below, springing from hundreds of small entrepreneurial efforts by the workforce, some of which work and form new directions the enterprise follows, and most of which fail and are not pursued any further. Many of the most successful enterprises, some of giant overall size, are, in fact, uncertain about how the whole thing works, such is the flexibility and emphasis on 'bottom-up' attitudes.

Hence, when we talk about *entrepreneurship* here, we do not mean the quality possessed by an inspired innovator like Henry Ford but a set of *functions* which may be taken by one person but more usually are carried out by a whole team of people, including, sometimes, everyone in the enterprise. Entrepreneurship is not an authoritarian function confined to and jealously guarded by top management and staff, but *an expression of human creativity by the entire enterprise.*

The link between entrepreneurship (in the wide sense defined above) and long-run productivity increases cannot be overemphasized. Productivity advance in Australia *must* emphasize the development of entrepreneurship (and the removal of obstacles to entrepreneurship), including the sharing of entrepreneurial functions within teams.

The first economist to focus on the entrepreneur as a key agent of productivity improvement was Richard Cantillon (1680–1734) who introduced the word 'entrepreneur' to the literature and described the uninsurable risks that he must bear, buying inputs at known prices and selling products at uncertain prices later. Jean B. Say (1767–1832) elaborated this theory further, stressing the entrepreneur's role in factor combination, risk bearing and continuing management. The concept of an identifiable entrepreneurial function subsequently pervaded continental European economic thought much more than the Anglo-Saxon tradition. The European, especially the Austrian, tradition has always seen entrepreneurship as an efficiency-enhancing activity of testing new solutions in a world of uncertainty and imperfect knowledge.

One European theory of entrepreneurship that is still influential is the sociological theory of Max Weber (1864–1920), who described how religious motivations induced exertion, ordering and accumulation, and facilitated the rationalization of the production process — activities he saw as crucial to productivity growth.

Another European model of entrepreneurship was that of Joseph Schumpeter (1883–1950) who saw the entrepreneur as a heroic, atavistic type with the willpower to overcome obstacles in the way of higher productivity and new products, who perceived opportunities and made the technical and organizational changes necessary for getting new knowledge to work. Schumpeter — like Karl Marx before him — saw the revolutionary role of the entrepreneur, but — unlike Marx — stressed the *ongoing* process of creative destruction in which old processes and products are superseded and in which capitalism rejuvenates itself.

More recent theory would include the ideas of David McClelland (1961), who might be categorized as a neo-Weberian. McClelland introduced family socialization and education and the intermediate psychological motive of 'achievement need' into Weber's theory of socio-psychological motives triggering entrepreneurial effort. McClelland's experiments in motivating and educating entrepreneurs are worth noting, despite the fact that he focused on developing countries (McClelland et al., 1969).

Another modern theory worth noting for the Australian context is that of Everett Hagen (1962). Hagen showed that traditional social structures may lead to the emergence of many creative entrepreneurs from the ranks of 'out groups', those who have experienced 'status withdrawal' and who overcome their initial tendencies to retreat. Migration to a new country is an act of 'status challenge', one that can make immigrants and their descendants entrepreneurial. Recent historical instances of 'status withdrawal' have been the downfall of the Togukawa in Japan which made the samurai into economic entrepreneurs, the defeat of Germany in 1945 which turned the well-trained officer corps into the agents of the German 'economic miracle', and the expulsion of the Kuomintang from the Chinese mainland to Taiwan. There may be considerable promise for Australia in Hagen's model (and considerable implications for multicultural policy!).

Also, it is worth noting the theory of Gus Papenek (1962) and others, who stress that there is always a *potential* supply of entrepreneurs, but that, in many societies, this supply is blocked by obstacles — insufficient demand, resource bottlenecks (e.g. import controls), inflation (which increases entrepreneurial risks and offers non-productive but lucrative speculation opportunities), adverse taxation policies, regulation, political instability and insecurity about property rights (see also Aubrey, 1955; Baumol, 1968). This theory is complemented by the entrepreneurial theories of Harvey Leibenstein (1968), and Albert Hirschmann (1958), who focus on how genuine entrepreneurs overcome these obstacles to better efficiency.

Finally, we have the 'hearts and minds' theories of Weisskopf, Bowles and Gordon (1983), Peters and Waterman (1983), and others, who see the entrepreneurial function as responding to the social arrangements *within enterprises* as well as within the society. Their message is that if people know that they count as real people in their work, rather than as robots or cogs, they behave with all the creativity and enthusiasm and entrepreneurship that is natural in human beings and which they show in non-work activities under their own control and choice.

Entrepreneurial risks vary considerably of course, depending on the industry and depending on the role that a firm chooses for itself in a given market. There is frequently a range of choice for firms about taking an aggressive or a defensive stance in their dynamic relationships with competitors. The stance chosen depends on the assessment of the expected rewards (profits) and costs of aggression or defence. Many markets may change from phases of aggressive activity to phases of 'defensive peace'. If all rivals satisfy average profit goals and no one has to fear the risk of outsiders appearing on the scene, few innovative (aggressive) moves have to be risked to maintain each rival's market niche. If such a state of defensive peace prevails for long, risk-averse values permeate the attitudes of the rivals and become dominant in the formulation of each firm's objectives. The more entrepreneurial managers will be 'selected out'. Such personnel selection creates self-perpetuating unenterprising patterns. Likewise, an experience of success in risky, innovative moves creates a sociological selection process that filters entrepreneurial and challenge-seeking values into the objectives of firms and among their top management.

Mescon and Vozikis (1982) argue that risk-taking is now almost exclusively the domain of small business and quote Norris (1976) on the growing 'no-risk' culture in the USA:

> The rising cost of innovation, investor pressure for immediate earnings, and greater economic uncertainty have accentuated the tendency of large corporations to avoid the risks associated with truly innovative products or services ... but big business is not alone. It shares its apathetic, risk-avoiding, selfish and reactionary profile with other sectors, including academia, organised labour, private foundations, the churches and government.

As we have noted earlier, insurance against uncertainty reduces the ability to deal with it. Firms concentrating on achieving government protection for their position or on forming defensive cartels among themselves will lose the capacity to respond to challenges through their own efforts. 'Micro-stability' (an unchanging structure of activities within each enterprise) yields a situation of 'macro-instability' (a failure of the capacity to maintain the viability of the enterprise as a whole). 'Macro-stability' requires a willingness to accept 'micro-instability' (changing the structure of activities within the firm). This rule applies at the level of the economy as well. The appropriate policy response to achieve 'macro-stability' (the ability to stay competitive) either for firms or the economy as a whole is to encourage the structural changes necessary in firms or the economy as a whole. This process will itself alter dominant value structures from defensive (leading ultimately to collapse in the face of the ever-mounting, unforeseeable changes in the world) to entrepreneurial (leading ultimately to persistent success in dealing with the impact of the unforeseen). As Klein (1977, p. 42) notes:

> In fact, the main advantage of a capitalist society based on decentralised risk-taking over a socialistic-society based upon

centralised planning is the ability of the former to 'internalise risk'. Risks are said to be internalised when the incentives favour *dealing with* an uncertainty in order to reduce it rather than ignoring the uncertainty. For example, when a firm *deals with* a technological uncertainty in order to escape from competitive risk, 'risk internalisation' occurs. Without a mechanism to internalise risk a society based upon centralised planning cannot hope to achieve the same degree of *dynamic* efficiency as a society that provides genuine incentives for the internalisation of risk ... In order to be good borrowers (of technology) firms must be highly flexible. For example, Japanese firms are highly flexible borrowers, which is to say, they are very good at reacting to negative feedback (which means they must be exposed to internalisation of risk — they could make serious losses).

If industries which have enjoyed a state of unenterprising reproduction of old market patterns year after year are confronted with a challenge for change, they will frequently, then, have 'unlearned' the capacity to cope. Mechanisms of quick constructive response, of parrying market challenges, have to be practised and valued. If they are not there, the natural tendency of the unenterprising manager is to seek direct protection from the new competition, normally by using connections and influence to secure government help. This may offer temporary reprieve but, in the long run, only constructive, productivity-enhancing responses will secure markets and jobs. The history of political protection of outdated, low-productivity jobs — from Tibetan lamaseries to the Australian textile industry — speaks a clear language: in the face of new technical and economic trends, governments are not capable of preserving jobs. *Only the constructive entrepreneurial response of innovative enterprise can protect jobs and living standards.* Firms frequently face a choice between the high risks of productivity-raising innovations that break completely new paths and promise great profit — and the lesser risks of imitating the productivity leaders. Indeed, most firms are imitators most of the time and not heroic, pioneering, path-breaking innovators. But, in imitating successful pioneers, they fulfil two important social functions. First, they diffuse newer, more productive technology and thus raise the average productivity level of their industry. Second, they increase the availability of products and services produced with the more productive technology and thus help to compete away the initially high profits of the pioneers. This ensures that 'pioneer profits' do not last for ever and that buyers ultimately get the benefits of higher productivity in the form of lower prices.

It must be realized that entrepreneurship is a tender plant which does not grow easily in hostile climates. Social hostility to profits (reflected, for example, in taxation policies) or the presence of major risks (such as the breakdown of the rule of law) may lead to a suppression of entrepreneurship and innovation or to a channelling of entrepreneurial energies into purposes other than productivity advance. Many traditional societies — like the advanced societies were before the industrial revolution or like the present less developed countries — are in that state. Profitability is then insufficient for entrepreneurs to overcome the obstacles and risks to innovation and enterprise. Such societies work without much change in production technology. Their income is static, or may even decline.

Compared to many other modern industrial societies, Australia has — in the post-war period — had many of the traits of such traditional societies. Our economic growth has been weak not because we have not worked hard enough or because we have not saved enough, *but because we have had so little aggressive enterprise, and innovation, using new skills, and new knowledge* (Kasper et al., 1980). Australia will only gain accelerated productivity growth if many more people take the risks of new approaches to production. In fact, if many entrepreneurs are innovating at the same time, they are likely to create the conditions for their collective success — entire complexes of interdependent innovations will develop that create dynamic market growth for everyone. Such a situation of rapid and mutually reinforcing innovation produces conditions in which costs start falling generally throughout the economy due to so-called 'external economies'. This makes for faster changes in production in the economy as a whole, and is a pre-condition for inflation-free rapid growth. If we have inflation-free growth, more entrepreneurial talent is pointed away from speculation and towards further efforts to enhance productivity.

A series of research studies which would be very helpful for Australia in this context would include first, a number of intra-industry case studies of Australian industry, analysing what makes for productivity leaders and laggards within each industry. There are many inspiring yet generally unknown industrial success stories in Australia, and the secrets of their success are worth compiling for the benefit of others. Second, a number of inter-industry comparisons between Australian industries, and between the same industries in other countries would be useful to illuminate differences in the degree of competitive rivalry and their effects on productivity growth in those industries. Third, it would be interesting to have several historical studies of entrepreneurial behaviour (and its social context) which laid the basis for fast productivity growth, for example, during the Meiji period in Japan, in Germany after the First World War, Taiwan and Singapore in the 1960s, and present-day China.

5 The Organization Of Work and Productivity Advance in the Workplace

In our view, this area is in many respects the key area for research on productivity advance. The social and political relationships involved in the organization of work undoubtedly govern the rate and nature of technological advance, the quality of work produced, the flexibility of enterprises which permits macro-stability (i.e. long-term economic viability). We hold that the quality of work life, in the sense of the degree of autonomy and 'self-actualization' achieved by individual workers, is an integral part of the productivity equation.

It is widely recognized in the United States, and now rapidly becoming so in Australia, that dynamic success in an enterprise requires a quite different strategy from static success, i.e. success in a certain, unchanging environment. In an uncertain world, the dynamic paradigm of survival — and success — of an enterprise depends on *evolutionary capacity*, the capacity to accommodate to the unforeseen, to sail on the shifting socio-economic winds rather than trudge relentlessly on to defeat. This ability to adjust to the winds and currents requires a shift to values which are far removed from those informing the grand design, the *idée fixe*, of the rationalistic planners. It requires an emphasis on the autonomous, self-actualizing contributions of all persons in an organization and especially at the grass roots. It requires 'bottom-up' rather than 'top-down' values. Control is exercised by maintenance of the values of the organization by the upper management, who also sift the experiments flowing from the shop floor which form the diversity of material from which successful evolution occurs. These organizations are 'people-oriented', encourage trying and making mistakes, at the grass roots have simple, informal but intense communications, and encourage action rather than deliberation.

The style of such enterprises is one of 'structured chaos' — chaos from the dynamic experimentation, and autonomy at the grass roots, 'structured' by personal understanding of, and sharing in, the values and purposes of the enterprises. This form of organization does not pretend to know what will succeed, but places its reliance simply on the genius of all its employees to create a sufficient flow of opportunities, improvements and ideas from which 'winners' can continuously be fashioned. The emphasis on the grass roots leads to an emphasis on small basic operating units: teams of ten or so people and plants of not more than 500 to 1000 in size (Peters and Waterman, 1983). The dynamic importance of 'the grass roots' is emphasized over and over in the literature.

For example, Rosenbloom and Abernathy (1982), in a study of the consumer electronics industry, suggest that these internal considerations of organization, values, and leadership predominate over external factors in explaining differences in innovative behaviour. Similarly, Ranftl et al. (1977) discuss the findings of the Hughes Corporation Report which examined major US companies and organizations. The findings were that means for improving productivity are unique to each organization and the set of individuals within it — there is no procedural 'magic bullet' which will do the trick, only principles whose implications have to be worked out anew for each organization. Professional management and high productivity are inseparable. The main path to improved productivity is through effective management and leadership which sets in place high operating standards, a creative environment, strong people-orientation, effective communication, cost consciousness, and simplicity in all operations (Ranftl et al., p.25). Ranftl suggests the following profile as typical of a highly productive organization:

Profile of a highly productive organization

1. The organization is effectively staffed and is people-oriented. Without these qualities it has virtually no chance of achieving high productivity.
   Typical observations:
   - Has effective and respected management/leadership
   - Has outstanding personnel in key positions
   - Has strong internal resources from which to draw
   - Uses people to the best of their abilities — matches the assignment to the individual
   - Provides the proper opportunities, assignments, and performance feedback necessary for personal growth
   - Respects employees and their individual differences
   - Is sensitive and responsive to employees' concerns
   - Keeps employees informed
   - Has an effective system of recognition and reward for achievement

2. The organization has high standards. A reputation for high technical and managerial ethics is the hallmark of a productive R&D organization.
   Typical observations:
   - Has high standards of operation, and stresses personnel and product integrity
   - Is performance/schedule/cost/quality/reliability conscious, maintains high standards of achievement in these areas
   - Maintains justice and equity in all operations
   - Continually strives to improve operations

3. The organization operates in a sound, competitive manner. Prudent business operation and a readiness to perform and compete are necessary for productive enterprise.
   Typical observations:
   - Has clearly established, worthwhile goals
   - Is profitable and a strong business sense prevails
   - Maintains a balanced capability which is sufficiently broad in scope to assure stability
   - Meets its goals/commitments — consistently gives timely responses — can be counted on
   - Is totally committed
   - Lives within budgets
   - Keeps costs under control
   - Requires accountability
   - Maintains a sound business backlog
   - Affords reasonable organizational growth or at least relative stability
   - Responds quickly and effectively to emergencies

4. The organization has a creative and productive atmosphere. In the R&D environment, factors that are conducive to creativity also tend to stimulate productivity.
   Typical observations:
   - Is dynamic, flexible, adaptive, and free of stifling controls
   - Encourages innovation and the taking of calculated risks
   - Furnishes a continual flow of meaningful and challenging assignments
   - Maintains effective communication among colleagues
   - Provides up to date technological aids, equipment and facilities

5. The organization has a 'can do' attitude and a high esprit de corps. The enthusiasm, dedication and teamwork of the people in an organization can never be underestimated as key factors in achieving optimal productivity.
   Typical observations:
   - Employees exhibit a genuine sense of commitment and a determination to perform
   - Employees have a strong team spirit — they enjoy their jobs and are proud of their contribution to the team
   - Team members depend on each other rather than compete with each other — they exhibit strong interpersonal trust
   - Employees have confidence that management fully supports them and their efforts
   - The organization exhibits mature confidence in the face of difficult situations — does not panic
   - Employees have strong organizational loyalty

Source: Ranftl et al. (1977)

Gillett and Ashkenas (1981) also argue that management should involve employees directly in solving problems and proposing actions, as employees are usually a rich source of insights into how to do a job better. In developing their ideas, employees become more committed to goals and develop a 'can do' attitude. The key to tapping the productivity potential of a firm is to focus on results, providing clear leadership by managers, but involving employees. It is clear that this strategy has been widely accepted as the road to rapid productivity growth, even in unlikely countries such as China under the Communists, where the strategy of decentralization, deregulation, small-group responsibility and market co-ordination has been adopted at the highest levels of the Party. As Chi-liang Yang (1981) notes, the solution (in China) is to make individual groups responsible for costs and profits in their own enterprises.

An interesting historical example of management creating an atmosphere conducive to change is provided by Peters (1978). He examines Owen's spinning mill in Scotland during the years 1800–1825. Two choices for technological change were open to Owen. Either he could bring it about by threats if workers did not co-operate; or he could change the workers' attitude through a change in work conditions. Owen chose the latter. He guaranteed jobs despite the (then) American trade embargo, thus winning the support of his employees for a number of innovations. A modern parallel cited by Peters is Japanese enterprises offering lifetime employment. Workers in those firms accept and welcome technological change, knowing their continued employment is not in doubt. This leads to greater workforce flexibility, which Peters suggests is a 'more reliable and cost-effective source of greater productivity than the introduction of new technology'. If security is provided, faster productivity advance becomes more feasible.

This finding is confirmed by Dymmel's (1979) study of the US telephone industry. Dymmel found that policies of retraining and non-replacement of labour which minimize worker displacement resulted in technological change being more readily accepted by telephone industry employees. This finding also shows the difference in solutions to problems as seen by dynamic analysis compared with 'static' analysis. Layoffs are indicated to be appropriate by static analysis, when labour requirements decline: but no layoffs is the appropriate policy according to dynamic analysis, because this strategy makes technological change more acceptable, and productivity advance is then faster than it would otherwise have been.

Unions also can contribute positively to productivity advance.

For example, Addison and Barnett (1982) argue that by providing workers with a 'voice' at the workplace unions can affect positively the way firms behave, enabling management to learn more about, and improve the operation of, workplaces and production processes. Freeman and Medoff (1979) conclude (from US evidence) that productivity may be higher in unionized than in (otherwise comparable) non-unionized work settings. Brown and Medoff (1978) also find a positive correlation between unionization and productivity in US manufacturing. They offer three alternative explanations: better labour quality in unionized than non-unionized firms, or unions organizing in the most productive firms, or unionization making firms more productive.

However, Elbaum and Wilkinson (1979) disagree with this conclusion. Their evidence for the British steel industry suggests that the union's success in maintaining control of tonnage rates made a significant contribution to the industry's lack of competitiveness. Similarly, in another study of British industry, Lazonick (1979) compares the cotton spinning industry with its American counterpart. He concludes that greater management-union conflict in Britain plays a role in the lower level of productivity in Britain compared with the USA.

What is overwhelmingly clear, however, is that within-enterprise productivity advance is fostered by employee participation combined with material work incentives. For example, Cable and Fitzroy (1980) conclude from a statistical analysis of West German data that worker participation and profit sharing have a positive effect on productivity, a finding consistent with Jones' (1983) analysis of a quite different work environment — Polish producer co-operatives.

Changing managerial practices

One of the most important responses to declining productivity growth in the United States over the last decade has been the change in managerial attitudes and job practices. Traditionally, the United States has been the home of 'scientific management'. Its mass production technologies, its business schools, and its corporate management philosophies have been envied and emulated. The classic way to encourage productivity growth at the level of the individual firm was seen as the better use of capital, more effective marketing strategies, applications of advanced technology, and more efficient management techniques. The principles of scientific management were set out by Frederick Taylor at the beginning of this century. The essence of Taylorism is that manual operations could be reduced to a set of motions in which the worker would interact with machine and materials in the one 'best' way. The role of management was to plan, measure and direct this mode of production; the role of labour was to carry it out, with little or no discretionary decision-making.

A vast body of production engineering knowledge has grown out of the attempt to reduce manual and clerical operations to a minimum set of procedures. It is no exaggeration to say that Taylorism has dominated industrial practice as part of mass production technology in the West. The Organization and Methods (O&M) expert, or the time and motion man standing over assembly line workers with his stop-watch, has become a figure instantly recognizable in cartoons and jokes about factory life. The organization theory taught to managers during this period has held that responsibility for problem-solving should be delegated to the lowest level of the organization competent to take such responsibility. Few could quarrel with that. The crucial point, however, is that it was only the lowest level of *management* which was regarded as competent to make decisions.

A substantial change has come about in the USA in the last decade. The organization is now seen as a social system over which management has, and can only ever have, partial control. How the whole system performs, therefore, depends on the autonomous behaviour of all the employees within it. This has often been recognized in the rhetoric of management in the past, but has not informed their actual behaviour. As Rosow (1979, p.29) puts it:

> Ask any businessman what the key factors are in *productivity*. The answer without exception is: capital, technology and manpower. That is what they *say*. Their actions, however, reveal their true concerns: capital and technology, period. Manpower drops out of the equation ... Catch a businessman in an unguarded moment and enquire what — if anything — he plans to do about productivity growth. If he mentions seeking increased co-operation from his workforce, you have found a pearl-bearing oyster ... The role of labour in productivity growth is so fundamental, so obvious, that managers stare right past it.

A major reason for this, we believe, is that conventional economic theory gives very little importance to the social and industrial relations of production. Production is regarded as a harmonious transformation of inputs into outputs, with all participants sharing the same interest of securing maximum output (Edwards and Nolan, 1983). Nelson (1981) maintains that conventional economic theory promotes two assumptions: 'that technological knowledge is the basic determinant of the input–output possibilities available to a firm' and 'that management "choice" among clearly defined options determines what a firm does'. The implicit image, continues Nelson, is of a firm as a machine, with some human parts. Management is in control, making decisions which are implemented through a hierarchical chain of command. Production is characterized as a set of technical relations, devoid of any specific institutional or social character.

This conception of production activity developed despite the evidence from the Hawthorne experiments in the mid-1920s that organizations were *not* like machines that could be tightly controlled by top managements. It became quite apparent from these and subsequent experiments that productivity is very closely related to worker attitudes and the structure and social relations of the work group. As we have noted earlier, *how workers feel about their job, fellow-workers, management and the organization may be more important in influencing productivity than the formal organizational structure or even financial incentives offered to employees* (Nelson, 1981).

A large body of contemporary research by economists into productivity has now cast considerable doubt on the concepts and assumptions of conventional theory. Pratten (1976), Caves (1980) and Prais (1981), for example, have drawn attention to the important link between productivity and industrial relations. Each of these writers, like others cited earlier, concludes that problems with labour relations have significantly contributed to Britain's poor economic performance. However, as Edwards and Nolan point out, their emphasis on the labour problem (being one of recalcitrant workers and trade unions) is quite misleading because it fails to explore the ways in which management, workers and unions have *together* constructed a social structure with specific sets of relations and expectations within the production process.

According to Edwards and Nolan, it is important to examine the dynamic interaction between the processes of industrial relations, work organization, industrial development and productivity. The manner in which trade unions have developed in Britain and Australia aptly demonstrates the importance of this dynamic process. Because their origins lie in the various craft occupations, trade unions draw their membership across industries, with very little identification with any one industrial sector. Consequently, the economic interests of the unions is predominantly at the level of improving the earnings of members, rather than at the level of the economic well-being of the particular industry or company, and its ability to accommodate wage increases (Wilson, 1982). This mismatch of economic interest has led to considerable mistrust and conflict between unions and management.

On the other hand, at the organizational level, the dynamic interaction between industrial relations, work organization and productivity does not necessarily reflect this broader conflict of economic interest. Workers are not merely concerned to minimize their level of effort in return for the highest possible wages. They also have an interest in such things as job security, promotion, social relationships, clean and safe working conditions, as well as doing meaningful work which gives them some satisfaction:

> Workers are adaptive and creative agents with a capacity for work which has to be transformed into actual labour through the social organisation of work. There are necessarily elements of co-operation and conflict in any production process. (Edwards and Nolan, 1983, p. 8)

Conventional economic theorists, together with their 'structural-functionalist' cousins in sociology, tend to place a great deal of emphasis on co-operation, and tend to regard conflict as an aberration. Their unitary frame of reference stresses the importance of shared goals and values in the industrial enterprise, whilst conflict, particularly when it takes the form of a challenge to managerial prerogatives, is viewed as dysfunctional and a threat to established authority.

'Left-wing' radical economists and sociologists, on the other hand, mistrust established authority structures and prefer to focus on goals and interests of sub-groups or social classes. The conflict of economic interest between workers and owners/managers is regarded as fundamental and all-pervasive, influencing all aspects of employee-management relations; and very little short of the overthrow of the capitalist system will mitigate this conflict.

Arguing from opposite sides of the political spectrum, these two schools of thought paint a distorted and incomplete picture of social reality. Both the conservative and radical perspectives have elements of truth, for there are indeed some goals and values shared by all society's members, and there are some goals and values which are exclusive to certain sub-groups or classes in society. Likewise, co-operation is just as constant a feature of all human society as is conflict, and neither should be regarded as an aberration or pathological condition.

According to Lenski (1966), social systems vary greatly in the degree of interdependence and integration of their parts. Distributive systems simultaneously reflect system goals and unit or sub-group goals, with each often subverting the other. Some organizations, for instance, may be highly cohesive, with insignificant levels of conflict, whilst others remain fragmented and divided by industrial conflict and strife. Social scientists, writes Lenski, should devote more attention to the causes and consequences of these variations in the degree of group integration.

This intermediate (or 'pluralist') position accepts that within any industrial enterprise there will be a variety of competing groups and individuals. As in the wider society, competing interests are maintained in some degree of equilibrium, with mutual recognition between the groups — management and unions, for instance. Conflict is not necessarily dysfunctional as it often leads to a more effective enterprise (Ford and Hearn, 1980).

Economists and social scientists are increasingly adopting this 'pluralist' position and thereby achieving new understandings of the links between industrial relations, work organization and economic performance:

> Instead of starting from a technical conception of production and then fitting conflict uneasily into this model, they see production as a social process and demonstrate how institutions grow up to express and contain this process and how institutions come to influence the range of choices which is available to the parties. (Edwards and Nolan, 1983, p. 10)

Australian management practices
Australian management has been amongst the most conservative in holding to the outmoded 'scientific management' perceptions of their task.

According to Pym, writing in the early 1970s, Australian managers are highly dependent on the ideas and practices of Europe and America. They are also unwilling to accept the need for change, they fear anyone who might threaten the established order through the introduction of radical alternatives, and they are dominated by 'sleepers' rather than 'thrusters'. After completing a study of private sector managers in five industrialized countries, G.W. England

(1975) concluded that Australian managers are paternalistic and have a conservative outlook which is resistant to any changes which threaten to disrupt long-established patterns of behaviour and authority. They also tenaciously defend managerial prerogatives and show very little enthusiasm for any expansion in influence of employees over decisions about the organization of work at the enterprise level.

A survey conducted by Sentry Holdings Ltd (1978) revealed that the majority of Australian managers in the sample supported the concept of involving employees in job-related decisions, but they were strongly opposed to any shift of power at the enterprise level from themselves to their employees. Three years later, Sentry Holdings (1981) conducted a further study to compare Australian managers with their counterparts in Japan, United States and United Kingdom. Australian managers were found to be less concerned about declining productivity and were less willing to make sacrifices in their life style to achieve economic growth. They also did not favour trade unions having a greater role in decision-making at either the enterprise or national level.

As a result of their research, Byrt and Masters (1974) drew up the following unflattering profile of the Australian middle manager:

> Dependent on government; insular; lacking in boldness and initiative; dependent on overseas sources for capital, ideas and techniques; reasonably but not highly educated; masculine in fact and outlook; conservative; fearful of radicalism in economics and politics; egalitarian both socially and at the work place; practical and pragmatic; opportunists rather than planners; non-intellectual — some are anti-intellectual; interested in leisure, social activity and family; critical of politicians and the holders of formal authority; versatile; materialistic; non-aggressive; manipulative in managerial style; low in Machiavellian characteristics.

The common theme which these researchers are uncovering is the deep-seated fear which Australian managers have of losing prerogatives in decision-making, together with doubts that workers can make worthwhile and constructive contributions, and concern that giving workers a voice will strengthen the union's bargaining position. For most managers, it is far easier and safer to operate as a traditional supervisor within a hierarchical organizational structure. Information can be controlled, options kept confidential, and criticism muted and channelled.

Unions have often been viewed as a vehicle for gaining greater worker input into workplace decision-making. However, unions generally have tended to react to management initiatives as they occur, rather than themselves initiating change. Many of Australia's 300 or more unions are very small, fragmented and occupationally-based and rely on the protection and recognition of the Conciliation and Arbitration Commission for their continued existence. Moreover, greater 'employee participation' poses a potential threat to the authority of unions and their grip on the voluntary support of members.

With their union representatives reluctant to lead the thrust for greater employee participation, workers are in a poor position to initiate change. Once outside the union fold, workers are relatively powerless and unorganized. Furthermore, there is little evidence that union leaders have misread the wishes of their members when they fail to place workplace reorganization high on their list of priorities. By and large workers are not visionaries who contemplate sweeping alternatives. Most learn to adjust to poor working conditions and authoritarian structures, and usually compensate through activities outside work (Alexander, 1983). In addition, high unemployment tends to smother worker concern over participation: getting and keeping a job takes precedence.

During the mid-1970s, Emery and Phillips (1976) conducted a survey of 2000 non-managerial employees across Australia. They found that people in highly bureaucratized jobs (those with most rigidly circumscribed work) were four times more likely to be dissatisfied than those who had jobs low on this dimension. Moreover, the greatest polarization between labour and management occurred in highly bureaucratized work environments.

The respondents who were most satisfied with their work had jobs which entailed greater variety of experience, opportunities for learning, mental challenge, and a desirable future. One of the main implications of the survey is the importance of job design and organizational structure to create the pre-conditions for work motivation, satisfaction and involvement. Commenting on these results, Lansbury and Spillane (1983) write (p.24):

> The implications of these survey findings for organisations in Australia are extremely disturbing. The low expectations of many employees about the experience of life at work have fuelled a self-fulfilling prophecy whereby little satisfaction is either sought or gained beyond the pay packet.

Thus, there is a huge backlog of change to be made up in Australia in the world of production and production engineering which still largely operates primarily on Taylor's turn-of-the-century principles. Throughout this century the jobs of both blue- and white-collar workers have been steadily reorganized to adapt to technological change and the demands of mass production. Tasks have been broken down into their smallest components and workers have found themselves engaged in simple, repetitive actions which require very little thought. External design control, task specialization, repetition, de-skilling, individual financial incentives, minimal social interaction and close supervision are the work design principles which continue to dominate in spite of seventy years' social, technical and economic change.

The negative consequences of this approach, in terms of poor employee quality of work-life, low morale, industrial conflict and falling productivity levels have now been thoroughly documented (Emery and Phillips, 1976; Lansbury and Spillane, 1983; Hackman and Oldham, 1980 and Kriegler, 1980). When employees are given only basic and repetitive tasks to perform, with little opportunity to influence decision-making or develop their skills, and are rarely permitted to work without supervision, their jobs become boring, uncreative, lonely and inordinately tedious. Denied responsibility, challenge and initiative in their jobs, workers begin to lose interest in their work, their skills become eroded, they lose confidence in their abilities and become less committed to the goals of the enterprise.

However, the growing awareness of the link between quality of work-life, employee relations and productivity is now leading to a gradual movement in many parts of the industrialized world away from traditional managerial structures, towards more participative and flexible structures. Senior managers of companies are beginning to realize there are gains to be made through organizational change. At the same time, there are also a number of societal developments which are acting as a stimulus to greater employee participation. Traditional authority relationships generally are being questioned and are succumbing to rapid change (Gunzburg, 1979). This is evidenced by the growth of administrative appeals mechanisms, the appointment of ombudsmen, and passing of legislation on freedom of information. Local councils and government authorities are increasingly having to consult with members of the community likely to be affected by their actions. The nature of education is becoming more participative, with students and their parents obtaining increasing opportunities to become involved in representative bodies in their school. Young people entering the labour market are bringing new values to the workplace. A report by the Work in America Institute estimates that:

> ... ten years ago, 70 per cent of industrial workers were willing to accept managerial authority with minor reservations. Today, the reverse finding has emerged: younger, more educated workers resent authoritarianism. These jobholders have demanded, and to some extent received, greater autonomy in the workplace. (Yankelovich and Immerwahr, 1983)

Ironically, much of the change which has occurred in Australian companies is largely due to the success of northern European and Japanese competitors who have adopted employee participation programmes. Many Australian subsidiaries of European and Japanese companies have introduced the participative programmes operating in their parent companies. Philips and Mitsubishi are examples of this, and it is worth describing some of the changes which Philips has introduced.

Twelve years ago Philips in Victoria was experiencing severe staff problems and falling productivity levels. Management was increasingly concerned about inadequate quality control, poor labour relations and an unsettled workforce with low morale. Annual labour turnover was 120 per cent and the company faced significant tariff reductions.

Adopting the participative approach of its parent company in Holland, Philips' management held protracted discussions with its workers and their unions. They jointly decided that a massive work restructuring programme should be implemented. Radical changes to work methods, to the physical and social work environments and to the decision-making procedures in the factory were instituted.

The old production lines were a major source of dissatisfaction among the workers. Each operator was required to place a small number of electronic components in a television set which moved past on a conveyor belt. The work cycle was repetitious, required little skill and lasted only a few seconds. There was no freedom to move about and the pace of work was dictated by the line. Friction was often generated between operators, because a mistake by one person meant that the next in line had to correct it. Little social interaction was possible because of the layout of the line. Supervisors acted as overseers, controlling the workers.

Under the new system introduced, television assembly was

broken down into half a dozen or so major components, such as the cabinet, chassis, remote control panel and wiring. The old assembly lines were dismantled and workers formed themselves into small, self-contained production groups with a high degree of autonomy. These groups began to co-operate. Aided by engineers, they remodelled their work spaces. Some groups designed new production machinery, while others devised innovative production processes. They also monitored and controlled their own production output, levels of efficiency and product quality. As well as testing and fixing faults, the groups were also involved in training, hiring and firing.

Group members have become multi-skilled so they can work in different ways. They can choose to assemble the component entirely on their own (this requires a work cycle of about 30 minutes — a much longer time than any assembly operation under the old system), or alternatively rotate the individual tasks between group members. Stocks of each group's finished components are held in buffer storages. This makes each group less dependent on the activities of other groups.

The advantages of this type of assembly are twofold. Each worker is freed from the monotony of assembly line and now uses a wide range of skills and abilities. The company benefits because product quality is of a high standard and because work restructuring has allowed production to be flexible and thus highly responsive to market fluctuations. Under the old assembly line system, it took up to two days to change over from producing one television model to another. Semi-autonomous work groups, however, have created a multi-skilled workforce capable of changing from the production of 14-inch portable televisions to 26-inch remote-control models within minutes. This suits the small Australian market very well because manufacturers need to be able to produce relatively small batches of a wide range of products.

Under the recommendations of workers' committees, plant layout was redesigned to be cleaner, safer, more comfortable and attractive. Also, noise abatement devices, temperature control, improved lighting and ventilation were installed. Serious attempts were made to get away from a drab factory environment by allowing staff to redecorate their workshops. Pot plants and photographic murals have been purchased. Tennis and basketball courts have been built and so has a licensed club for all employees. Workers may take coffee breaks as frequently as they like.

Philips has also abandoned the traditional pyramidical organizational structure and introduced a structure which provides improved communication. Although the changes cost Philips a great deal for additional equipment and new technology, this outlay was quickly recouped by improved productivity. Before the change programme, the Melbourne plant was operating at 70 per cent efficiency, compared to other Philips' factories around the world. *Within one year of the change, this plant lifted its efficiency level to 120 per cent, making it one of the most efficient plants of its kind in the world.* Annual labour turnover dropped from 120 per cent to 20 per cent and absenteeism fell from 17 per cent to below 2 per cent, indicating a vastly improved level of worker satisfaction.

These results mirror precisely the substantial empirical evaluation of employee participation schemes carried out in the USA by Alber (1979), who surveyed 189 companies and six Federal government departments. Alber sought information on the financial outcomes of job enrichment programmes which had been introduced by the organizations. The research findings show that a variety of economic benefits flowed from job enrichment projects. The most often cited was increased production output, followed by increased job satisfaction, improved product quality (as measured by a decrease in items rejected for failure to meet quality standards), reduced labour turnover rates, reduced absenteeism rates, and reductions in the size of the workforce.

Crombie (1976) maintains that there are three basic reasons for introducing employee participation in the workplace; namely, as a means of job satisfaction, as a means of improving the effectiveness of organizations and, finally, as an end in itself, transforming society and improving the general quality of work-life.

Broadly speaking, there are two forms of employee participation: representative (or indirect) participation and direct participation. Representative participation provides for the participation of workers through their own representatives in various decision-making bodies of the enterprise. It may merely involve the addition of workers' representatives to existing boards or committees, or it may involve the creation of new structures such as works councils or consultative committees. This form of participation is sometimes called 'industrial democracy'. Direct participation, on the other hand, involves each worker in decisions at the workplace. The term usually implies the establishment of semi-autonomous work groups (as in the case of Philips) or the introduction of some form of job redesign or job enrichment. These two approaches are discussed in further detail below. Job enrichment increases task complexity by incorporating work stages normally done before and after the stage being redesigned; and gives each employee more responsibility for making the decisions that affect how the work is to be done. Workers may form teams with a considerable degree of autonomy.

Because participative structures vary enormously and can operate at various levels within the enterprise, debate about the concept is often confusing. Wang (1974) developed a descriptive matrix which provides a useful framework. His aim was to fit all the loose and technical terms into one simple model, thereby forming a base from which worker participation can be examined. As we can see in Figure 5, he views participation as a continuum which he breaks up into four categories — information sharing, consultation, joint decision-making and self-management. He also identifies the different decision levels as shop floor, departmental, organizational and corporate. These two sets of variables combine to form a matrix. A move up the matrix decreases the degree of managerial prerogative and increases the degree of attitudinal and structural change.

Autonomous work groups have two main features that distinguish them from traditional job structures: work is arranged around interdependent task groups undertaking longer more complete tasks rather than around discrete individual tasks, and control over tasks is located *within* rather than outside the group.

Cummings and Molloy (1977) suggest that the 'autonomous group' approach derives from a 'socio-technical systems' approach by the (London) Tavistock Institute of Human Relations. The notion of work as a socio-technical system follows from the fact that task performance requires both a technology (tools, techniques, and methods) and a social structure that relates people to the technology and to each other. Tavistock researchers were led to the explicit recognition of the interaction between technical and social systems by a coal-mining study carried out in the 1950s. In a series of writings, Trist and his colleagues (1951, 1963) noted that the shift from non-mechanized to mechanized mining created severe problems of task organization. Before the introduction of mechanized coal cutting and a conveyor system of transporting coal, miners worked in an individual task structure that coped well with the whole sequence of tasks involved. However, the newer form of mass-production mining separated the workers into three shifts. Workers who performed interdependent tasks became isolated; external supervision to integrate the tasks was not effective underground; productivity fell, and considerable tension developed between coal-face workers and supervisors.

Figure 5 Two-dimensional worker participation matrix

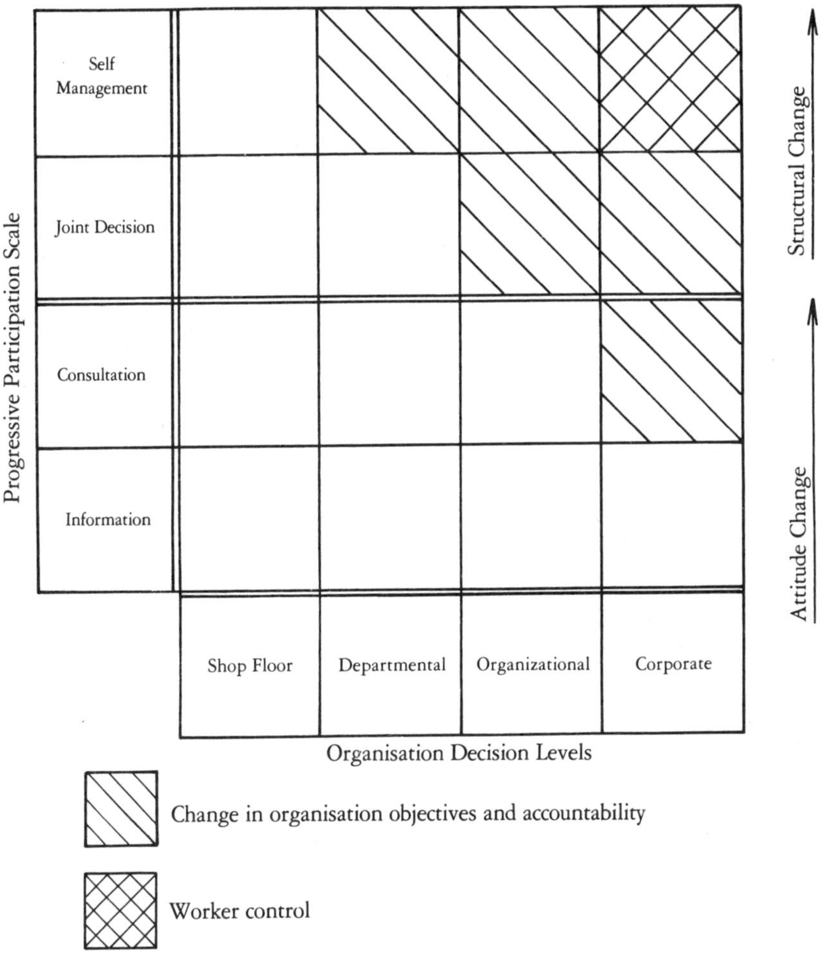

Organisation Decision Levels

Change in organisation objectives and accountability

Worker control

Source: Wang (1974)

The conclusion drawn from the Tavistock studies was that relatively autonomous groups of workers should take responsibility for a whole cycle of mining. It turned out not to be true that the new mechanized technology *imposed* a unique form of work design: different forms of social organization could operate the same technology equally effectively. The solution in the coal mining case was gratifying:

Based on self-selection and a common pay rate, group members adapted their task behaviour to match changes at the coal face. This resulted in increased productivity and reduced conflict and tension. (Cummings and Molloy, 1977, p. 22)

In summary, therefore, autonomous work groups may be seen as an attempt to structure the twin social and technical components of work into a jointly optimized system and to provide this system with the properties required for self-regulation. Such groups can offer at least two advantages over traditional, individually-based task designs. The first is the self-evident point that the steps involved in many production processes are interdependent. Grouping interdependent jobs facilitates the necessary interactions. The second advantage can be readily inferred from our earlier remarks on Taylor's 'scientific management'. The traditional method of breaking down production processes into their simplest parts and then specifying the behaviour of those parts requires an external control system to co-ordinate the separate parts. This control system itself requires co-ordination, which leads to a higher level control system, and so on.

The most comprehensive survey of autonomous work groups is by Srivastva et al. (1975) who charted the results of sixteen experiments in seven different countries and across such diverse types of work as key punching, assembly line, chemical process, and textile weaving. *In only one instance did productivity fall after the introduction of autonomous work groups: all others measured an increase. Moreover, these productivity improvements were generally accompanied by improvements in the quality of work performed, a reduction in absenteeism and turnover, and an improvement in measured attitudes towards job satisfaction and motivation.*

Walton (in Cummings and Molloy, 1977) describes the introduction of autonomous work groups at an American pet-food plant. The work is divided into largely self-managed teams, the size of each team (seven to fourteen people) being chosen to be large enough to include a 'natural' set of interdependent tasks but small enough for group co-ordination and decision-making. At the company's previous plant, individuals were permanently assigned to specific jobs. In the new scheme, assignments of individuals to specific tasks are subject to team consensus. Tasks can be shared, and they can be redefined by the team in the light of individual capabilities.

Most interestingly, each set of tasks (and each team) has designed into it what Walton calls higher-order human abilities and responsibilities. For example, activities that have traditionally been the role of separate maintenance, quality control or personnel departments have been devolved to the work groups. Each team member maintains the equipment he operates, and 'keeps house' in his own working area. Each team must perform its own quality tests and meet quality standards. Each team screens and selects employees to replace job leavers. Walton is in no doubt that the pet food manufacturer achieved 'a more reliable, more flexible, and lower-cost manufacturing plant, a healthier work climate, and learning that could be transferred to other corporate units', all at modest cost.

Car assembly lines are a by-word for routine, monotonous work, and the two autonomous work group experiments that created world-wide interest are the Saab-Scandia and Volvo plants in Sweden. Saab's truck assembly plant at Sodertalje has the following features:

1 assembly-line workers are members of 'development groups' that discuss tool and machine designs before they are introduced;
2 workers have been encouraged to learn several jobs;
3 as in the American pet-food plant, equipment maintenance has become part of the work tasks of assembly workers rather than being a separate, specialist function;
4 similarly, quality control has been shifted from a separate unit to individual production workers.

In 1972 Saab applied what it had learned from work groups in truck assembly to its new car engine factory. Again the key feature was that instead of a continuous production line, engines were assembled by relatively autonomous teams, each team having responsibility for a range of tasks. The ultimate objective was that each team member would learn to assemble an entire engine. As in the previous experiments we have mentioned, the company hoped for improvements in both productivity and worker satisfaction, the productivity gains stemming from less disruption to the production line, and reduced absenteeism and turnover.

The Volvo assembly plant at Kalmar has many similar features to the Saab-Scandia experiments. What is worth noting here is that the Kalmar plant, carefully designed for autonomous work teams which would have responsibility for particular sections of a car, was estimated to cost about ten per cent more than a conventional assembly line of comparable scale. (The main source of extra cost was the insertion of 'island systems' (buffer zones), which eliminated the conveyor pacing of work through the creation of free space, with buffer inventories between work stations.) Volvo justified the premium as 'another stage in the company's general attempt to create greater satisfaction at work'. This is no doubt very laudable, but it is also a signal reminder that quality-of-working-life enhancements may not come free. It is also possible that Volvo can be sanguine about a ten per cent premium: the particular Volvo product has a niche in the market which makes it relatively insensitive to this extra cost premium.

We noted earlier that job design is frequently based on the 'scientific management' principles that work is most productive when broken into simple constituent motions, and made repetitive, with minimum room for human judgement. The variety of schemes encompassed by the heading of 'job restructuring' have as their common denominator the questioning of this assumption. Just as the work of Trist at the Tavistock Institute provides much of the theoretical background to the introduction of autonomous work groups, so the research of Frederick Herzberg underpins the study of job restructuring. Herzberg suggests that satisfaction and dissatisfaction are not opposite poles of the same human feeling. A worker who is not dissatisfied is not necessarily satisfied: he may simply have no reason to complain. Herzberg's insight was to understand the positive contribution of motivation. To reduce dissatisfaction among workers does not guarantee that they turn into satisfied, motivated workers. Because dissatisfaction is reduced and a worker is not complaining about his job does not mean that he is motivated to do it well (Herzberg et al., 1959; Herzberg, 1966).

According to Herzberg, the causes of satisfaction or motivation are quite distinct from the causes of dissatisfaction. Dissatisfaction is determined by working conditions, pay, status of the job, supervision, company policy and interpersonal relations. These are clearly all aspects of the environment within which a person works. The sources of satisfaction are quite different, having more to do with the actual work itself: they include the nature of the work, the exercise of responsibility, opportunities for increased skill and competence, and the recognition of achievement.

The value of this insight is the implication that even an enlightened, considerate and benevolent management may fail to get good results from its workers. Such a management may well have a workforce with few grounds for dissatisfaction; but only by positive action on *job content* will it get a satisfied and motivated workforce. In short, to reduce dissatisfaction, improve the general environment; to increase motivation and satisfaction — and hence performance — improve job content.

Hackman and his colleagues (Hackman and Lawler, 1971; Hackman et al., 1975) have extended and elaborated Herzberg's work. Hackman measures the motivating potential of a job on five core dimensions:

1 skill variety — the degree to which a job requires the worker to perform activities that challenge skills and abilities;
2 task identity — the degree to which the job requires completion of a whole and identifiable piece of work;
3 task significance — the degree to which the job has a perceptible impact on the organization or outside;
4 autonomy — the degree to which the job gives a worker discretion in scheduling work and determining how it will be carried out;
5 feedback — the degree to which a worker is informed of the effectiveness of his work.

These five core dimensions of a job are alleged to create three critical psychological states:

1 experienced meaningfulness (individuals must perceive their work as worthwhile or important by a system of values they accept);
2 experienced responsibility (they must feel personally accountable for their efforts);
3 knowledge of results (they must be able to determine, on a regular basis, whether or not the outcomes of their work are satisfactory).

If these three conditions are present, people will be motivated to perform well.

Cummings and Molloy observe that over the last decade hundreds of job-restructuring projects based on Herzberg's theory have been published. They are also careful to note that the standard of experimental design has not been high. They quote Birchall and Wild (1973) who noted

... although a considerable number of experiments is reported, few show evidence of thorough experimental investigation. Little use was made of control groups for comparison. Only slight attention has been paid to the evaluation of benefits. Unsuccessful applications seem to have been forgotten.

It is therefore of considerable significance that even though they approach their survey of job restructuring with strong scepticism, they conclude with very favourable comments. They reviewed twenty-eight cases reported in the literature, and concluded that the most common effect of job restructuring was an improvement of attitudes (in 64 per cent of cases). Product quality improved in 61 per cent, productivity in 54 per cent, costs in 32 per cent, and absenteeism and turnover in 21 per cent.

Some flesh can be added to these skeletal figures if we turn to a particular case study. Walters (1982) describes job redesign at Citibank. A survey showed that Citibank rated very low on customer service, even though operating costs had risen 15 per cent a year for the past eleven years. Walters notes that

> ... a cast of thousands ... shuffled papers that were the basics of the 'transactions processing system'. These people were handling only a part of the whole, a single task over and over again. The repetitiveness of their work, and the fact that they had no sense of its completion, militated against consistently error-free performance. In fact, out of monotony or lack of attention, clerks tended to create errors in the processing flow.

The approach chosen by Citibank was the decentralization of operations so that one person provided a complete beginning-to-end service for a single customer. The actual process of job redesign leaned heavily on the work of Hackman and his colleagues. Walters terms the complete Herzberg/Hackman theory the 'theory of Motivational Work Design', and comments that this model was taught to all managers and supervisors at Citibank so that they could all contribute to the work redesign process.

Two concluding comments can be made about the Citibank experiment. The first is that there seems to be little doubt that productivity improved. Walters notes that the savings to Citibank 'show how changes in organisational and job structure, coupled with improved technology, can result in dramatic improvement'. The second comment is that the Citibank experiment is interesting because the introduction of new technology (mini-computers) was accompanied by demonstrable 'up-skilling' of the labour force, contrary to so much of what is heard in Australia. Ford has commented that Australia tends to follow British and American models of organizational behaviour, in which technology is seen as a way of de-skilling workers. In particular 'the failure to appropriately skill word processing operators and their clients has led to continued underutilisation of technology and people in so-called modern offices' (Ford, 1982, 1983). It is clear from the Citibank experiment that jobs *can* be redesigned around new technology so that skills and satisfaction are increased.

The debate in Australia concerning technological change has often been focused on its effects on job security, de-skilling and employment. Notification of impending change programmes and redundancy arrangements have tended to preoccupy much industrial relations activity. This is not in the least surprising because most managers regard technological change as a labour-saving process, which implies that the objective is 'to get rid of people'. This in turn implies that people are inherently unproductive, or certainly less productive than machines. When employees translate the notification of unilateral change as a sign that *their* labour is about to be saved and then refuse to co-operate, management often conclude that people can only hinder productivity, thus reinforcing management's commitment to labour-saving technology and processes.

In an address to the third annual Australia–Japan economic issues symposium, the Managing Director of Mitsubishi Motors Australia, Graham Spurling, maintained that Australian managers are far too ready to accept that technology and capital investment are the path to productivity and profitability. According to Spurling, it is pointless imposing high capital investment on an inefficient structure. He favours the Japanese approach which seeks to strain every resource to its limit before investing in high technology. Accordingly, Mitsubishi's philosophy is to get everyone within the organization — management and labour — working together to maximize the utilization of the existing plant before contemplating technological change. This, says Spurling, requires 'better organization and planning, better use of people, all the time tempered with mutual respect and understanding between manager and worker'. Through vastly improved industrial relations, work and organizational restructuring, and participative personnel practices, Mitsubishi was able to reduce the number of man-hours needed to build a car from 60 to 22 hours. Labour turnover has been brought down from 55 per cent to 12 per cent, and absenteeism from 9 per cent to 5 per cent. Workers' compensation payments have halved, and there has only been one minor industrial dispute in the past four years (Kriegler and Sloan, 1984; Kriegler, 1984).

In most discussion about technological change technology is seen as the determining factor in changing the work environment, skill levels and size of the workforce. In fact, new technology, depending on the way it is introduced, has the potential to either restrict or expand opportunities for employment growth, skill utilization, and quality of work-life.

Relying on purely technical solutions to production problems fails to take account of the fact that organizations are social systems. Bjorn-Anderson and Hedberg (1977), in a paper concerned with the designing of information systems in Scandinavian organizations, report that:

> Writers on design of information systems increasingly emphasize that changes in information technology should be planned in their organizational contexts, and that the whole spectrum of organizational needs should govern designing.

Bjorn-Anderson and Hedberg, however, lament that practice still diverges far from understanding of this crucial design principle. They report two Scandinavian case studies from the banking industry which fall well short of the socio-technical approach. In designing the computer systems for these banks, little attempt was made to restructure the organizational design or work roles. The design teams attempted to 'tailor the new information technologies to the existing organization and to make as few changes to work roles as possible'. But by neglecting the inherent relationships between the technical and the social systems, the design changes created a number of unintended social effects which were detrimental to the employees' output and work roles.

A similar situation occurred in Australia when Telecom introduced new switching technology, which was highly centralized and placed most employees in a maintenance (rather than an operations) role. In the new system the workers 'were required to accept increased workloads, less discretion, lower employment levels and technological change' (Muller, 1980). The Australian Telecommunications Employees Association (ATEA) responded with a proposal that responsibility for switching maintenance should rest with the district exchange (Tacy and Gough, 1982).

After a prolonged dispute the Arbitration Court decided that there should be a series of trials of both solutions, with independent experts using the following six criteria as a basis for evaluation: efficiency of operation, standard of service achieved, job satisfaction, career opportunities, maintenance of technical standards and retention of expertise, and public interest. The results of the trials were placed before the Commission, which decided to decentralize switching maintenance, with primary control over maintenance going to district exchanges and the State co-ordinating centres providing support.

Thus senior management's single-minded pursuit of new economic efficiency goals failed to take account of the *non-technical aspects* of the organization, thus provoking employee discontent. Like their Scandinavian counterparts, they failed to recognize that technology is merely one part of a total system. The introduction of technology, in other words, need not lead to a particular type of outcome in an inevitable progression. Indeed, current and emerging technology is undoubtedly the most versatile and flexible yet created.

Simpson is one of the largest manufacturers of whitegoods in South Australia. Over the past decade, technological change has played a vital role in the development of this company. In fact, Simpson has been a pioneer in the application of new technology in Australian whitegoods manufacture.

A combination of factors such as strong consumer demand and generous tariff protection during the 1940s and 1950s brought a large number of Australian manufacturers into the whitegoods industry. In the 1960s, the growth of the whitegoods market slowed considerably. The problem of excess capacity was further compounded by the growing number of imports entering the Australian market at this time. In response to growing competition from overseas products, most manufacturers sought further protection. By contrast, Simpson decided to rationalize and restructure its operations in order to achieve economies of scale and effectively compete on the international whitegoods market. The company's strategy revolved around product innovation, standardization of components, automation of assembly and sub-assembly processes, work redesign, and improved personnel practices.

Today, Simpson Holdings Limited is Australia's leading whitegoods manufacturer. It has five major whitegoods factories producing washing machines, clothes dryers, dish washers, refrigerators and freezers, and stoves. Over the past seven years, Simpson has progressively modernized and automated its factories, introducing high technology in the assembly of its products. The introduction of automation equipment into what once was a labour-intensive industry has reduced the number of people doing highly repetitive tasks on assembly lines. The workers operating the automation equipment are called multi-skilled assemblers or operators. They are given a high level of responsibility and they earn higher rates of pay than the normal assemblers. The machines they operate are cleaner, quieter and safer than the processes which they replaced.

A vital aspect of the Simpson drive to transform its factories to meet international standards was the policy of improving personnel practices. An important stage in this reorganization involved breaking the company into separate businesses, such as washing machines, dryers, dish washers, and so on. Each business now has its own management so that decision-making is delegated and, therefore, more effective because it is closer to the production processes and shop-floor workers.

Every month, the manager of each business is required by the corporation to meet with all the employees in that business. The meetings are held during work hours, and the manager is required to provide workers with a comprehensive report on the business. The briefings are frank and cover such things as the current state of the industry and the market, sales and production levels, profitability, proposed developments and the reasons for them, the cost of each new piece of equipment and its anticipated cost-benefit. Workers are expected to participate in these discussions, and to raise issues which they are concerned about. At these meetings, employees are also told about new products as well as any planned technological changes within the workplace. These issues are fully discussed and, wherever practicable, the employees most likely to be affected are invited to take part in the planning of these changes. Workers who are displaced by technological change or the introduction of automation equipment are not retrenched by the company. Simpson has a formal policy that retrenchments will not occur as a result of technological change or short-term economic fluctuations within the industry.

Generally, Simpson 'businesses' are broken down further into smaller sub-groups or work groups, each being responsible for a complete piece of work. The number of employees in the work groups varies, but usually does not exceed twelve. There are no formal consultative committees in the plants. Instead, there is a continuous cycle of group meetings which take place at all levels of the organization. Work groups, for example, operate with a high degree of autonomy. They are expected to make decisions for themselves and to resolve as many work-related problems as they can.

Since taking its radical decision, in 1974, to establish modern factories which would manufacture competitive products for both domestic and export markets, Simpson has remained committed to this strategy. Employment declined in the initial phases of the restructuring programme. Since then, however, employment growth has occurred in those products which became internationally competitive.

The clothes dryer plant was one of the first factories which Simpson upgraded to international standards. The plant became highly automated, using high-technology assembly and sub-assembly procedures, combined with microprocessor quality control systems. Productivity rose sharply as production runs increased. Economies of scale were achieved, allowing the products to compete successfully on the world market. Today, Simpson has acquired the major share of the Australian clothes dryer market, and significant export markets have been established. Since 1974, the price of Simpson dryers has risen at a rate well below the consumer price index. Furthermore, with expanding markets and mass production, the plant has significantly increased the size of its workforce (Kriegler and Sloan, 1984).

The practice of involving workers in the introduction of new technology used not to be very widespread in Australia even a few years ago, but the evidence suggests that the practice is now rapidly increasing. In Table 6, we compare the findings of two surveys — the first conducted in 1979 by the Working Environment Branch of the Department of Science and Technology, and the second, by the National Institute of Labour Studies in 1983. Although the questionnaires used by the two research bodies were very differently constructed, it is possible to broadly compare the data. The 1979 study found that 27 per cent of employers did not even let their employees know that they were about to introduce technological change. The 1983 survey, also conducted on a nationwide sample, revealed that only 10 per cent of firms failed to inform their employees. Compared with 27 per cent in 1979, 61 per cent of

Table 6 Changing levels of participation in the introduction of technological change

	Dept of Science and Technology 1979 %	National Institute of Labour Studies 1983 %
No information provided to employees	27	10
Employees received prior information about change	73	90
Employees and management discussed the change	27	61
Employees and management jointly decided *what* technological change should be introduced and *how* it should be effected	9	36
Employees were given total responsibility to decide what technological change should be introduced	0	9
	N = 288	N = 153

employers in the 1983 survey discussed the implications of the change with their employees, which suggests a massive increase in awareness, by employers, of the advantages and benefits of introducing consultative processes in the workplace. The most significant change of all occurred in the use of joint decision-making mechanisms. Whereas only 9 per cent of employers, in 1979, stated that workers and management *jointly decided* the nature of the technological change to be introduced as well as the method of its introduction, some 36 per cent of employers, in 1983, used this approach.

Whatever consultative mechanisms do, and their activities vary widely as we have seen, they all have some things in common. They provide workers with the regular opportunity to participate in decision-making, especially on the shop floor where their work is most directly affected. They help management at all levels to identify and solve problems facing the organization. They also provide a valuable learning experience for all employees on the structure and operation of the enterprise and the way in which each person relates to it.

It will be apparent to anyone familiar with the literature on workplace organization that our survey here has done little more than scratch the surface of the possibilities in dynamic productivity advance through changing socio-political workplace relationships. Nonetheless, the survey is sufficient to allow us to draw the conclusion that there is vast scope for research into productivity in the workplace. We suggest that the concept of the organization as a social system provides the unifying rationale for a cluster of investigations into increasing company productivity. Studies which we would give high priority to are the following.

First, a survey of the managerial literature on enterprises as social systems is called for. It is not difficult to see that at least part of the practical interest in these ideas has grown out of the impact of Japanese manufacturing methods on various American industries. The social organization of Japanese factories has been, to most Western eyes, at least as important in their export success as their skill in introducing and adapting new technology. If the social systems concept were simply a misguided attempt to import culturally inappropriate policies then it could be dismissed as a 'quick fix' reaction to low productivity growth. But there is more to it than that, as we tried to show in our description of the theory underlying autonomous work groups and job redesign. The full scope of the *theories* underlying the social system approach must be brought together and made accessible to an Australian audience.

Second, we urge a survey of American and European evidence on the dynamic effects on productivity in practice of reorganizing work along social system lines. Here, too, the examples we cited earlier are only a fraction of the total picture. The focus would not simply be yet another literature survey, but an attempt to pluck from overseas those principles and practices which could be *operational* in this country, and which would lead to organizational structures likely to be dynamic, evolutionary successes in the Australian environment.

Third, we should not allow our cultural cringe to show too prominently. There must be sufficient Australian examples of successful social systems reorganizations of work places to warrant analysis. For example, not a little of Ford's recent success in overtaking GM-H for market leadership has been the way in which Ford management, unions, and workers have co-operated to improve quality control — traditionally a Ford weakness. The details of this case and many like it should be publicized.

Fourth, we have already mentioned that at least some of the new American interest in work innovations derives from Japanese industrial success. Ford (1983) has usefully commented:

> It is innovation in Japanese production methods, organisational learning systems and planning that is consistently driving Western enterprises and industries to the wall. Continuous, incremental, and participative change is a characteristic of Japanese production processes ... In Japan, the idea of learning systems is fundamental to the development of organisational policies and practices. For instance, whereas the concept of job rotation in Australia is predominantly an imported personnel policy gimmick to move people between dull and boring jobs, in Japan it is a concept for systematically multiskilling employees.

It would be as silly to believe that Australia could import Japanese practices in turnkey fashion as it would be to throw in the towel and say it comes 'naturally' to Japanese because of their particular cultural background and is impossible to adopt here. What is required is careful study of company productivity in Japan, precisely to see what elements of it could be relevant and useful in Australia — and, though we talk of Japan, such an exploration ought to be comparative, including all the newly-industrializing countries of East and South-East Asia. Taiwan and South Korea are ex-Japanese colonies; Singapore and Malaysia make no secret of the fact that they are attracted by the Japanese rather than British or American models of industrial organization ('look East, young man'). As a result, all the rapidly growing countries of Asia display many 'Japanese' character-istics in their participative industrial organization, their styles of management and management education, their school systems, and their policies for worker training.

Finally, it would be useful to explore what changes in the institutional environment outside the enterprise would assist the social systems reorganization of enterprises. This focus provides a positive objective for unions, arbitration authorities and govern-ments to consider in evaluating proposals for change that arise from time to time.

Summary and Conclusions

We have argued that Australia is suffering not so much from a 'real wage overhang' as from a 'productivity underhang'. Australian productivity growth is weak in international terms. To correct this situation requires a deep appreciation of the fundamental sources of productivity growth — the socio-economic structures and attitudes which govern the rate of innovation in the economy. This book attempts to pinpoint the essential aspects of the social processes involved in achieving a dynamic, evolutionary economy.

There is a whole family of productivity concepts and measures relevant for various purposes. Productivity in its most general sense means the physical volume of output that is achieved from a physical volume of inputs. Because output is made up of many goods and services of altering qualities, prices and composition; and because inputs are made up of many factors which are difficult to quantify and which also alter in qualities, prices and composition, there is no unique, always-achievable best measure of productivity.

Productivity advance emerges as a result of social processes which condition a society's capacity to enhance the more proximate sources of productivity growth. That is why productivity advance is difficult and there are no 'quick fixes'. Australian productivity has been slow-growing because of Australian social arrangements.

There is a need, therefore, for the promotion of a broader public understanding of the basic economic and social principles underlying productivity advance. We have dealt with these under four major headings: the role of government, the effect of the general socio-economic environment and market structures, and the organization of work.

There is now widespread evidence that many government regulations have had adverse economic impacts quite outweighing their benefits. For example, studies of electricity generation in the US, public transportation in Chicago and Adelaide, railroads in

Canada and the US, and airlines in the US and Australia, find that higher productivity and a revitalization of small business activity often results from deregulation. Government regulation diverts managers' attention from entrepreneurial concerns such as product development, production and marketing: research and development can become largely 'defensive'. Government regulatory activism can seriously disrupt long-term investment plans of firms and create a climate of uncertainty unfavourable to investment.

Deregulation induces apparently chaotic, but highly innovative, services in place of lumbering, moribund monoliths. Policies that work through market processes are more likely to sort winning from losing innovations than government attempts to 'pick winners'. A reasonable prospect of profit and need to grapple with *uncertainty* are major incentives for technological change, and these conditions are best provided for by market structures intermediate between monopoly and 'atomistic' competition.

Technological change involves three stages — invention, innovation and diffusion. Invention seems to be dominated by individuals. Innovation is more complex. Major corporate R&D is important, although in some industries small firms have advantages. Strong, in-house R&D, close attention to users' needs, good communications with the scientific world and with customers, and patenting possibilities all play some role in innovation. Diffusion speed depends on social factors, profitability and capital requirements. Large firms seem to adopt innovations faster, while direct investment is the most important vehicle for international transfer of technology.

Australia's performance in R&D and innovation has been weak. Entrepreneurial attitudes and a supportive social environment need to be strengthened if our rates of innovation are to be raised. This is best done through the pressure of competition, regarded as a dynamic process of economic rivalry. Firms compete with each other to create, expand and defend 'market niches' by creating new products and processes which insulate each firm's pricing behaviour from excessive pressure by rivals. Because competitive pressure on one's market niche is uncomfortable, established producers often use their lobbying powers to obtain a government umbrella for their niche, which then removes both the pressure to innovate for defensive purposes and the incentive to innovate for expansion purposes. Cartels, and government-licensed or -regulated oligopoly markets, are likely to be ill-adapted to change, therefore; markets which are 'contestable' are likely to be innovative, and exhibit fast productivity growth.

Economies of scale are not a genuine hindrance to Australian firms achieving levels of productivity comparable with those in other advanced economies. The concerns about economies of scale arise from confining attention to the protected domestic market rather than the world market. Further, Australian monopoly producers will behave dynamically so long as the domestic market remains contestable. In addition, in a dynamic world, economies of scale are much less important than is popularly supposed: the need to be flexible in the face of uncertainty gives an advantage to small, nimble production units.

The quality and extent of entrepreneurial activity is also critical and depends in turn on the degree of market rivalry between firms. Entrepreneurship is an activity directed at dealing with the disequilibrium which firms continually face in a dynamic market. The function of the genuine entrepreneur is to deal with market relationships, political and human relations, control functions and technical management in a creative and innovative way which is critical for rapid productivity advance. This function appears to work best when decentralized throughout the enterprise. Team work and team attitudes are important elements in a thriving entrepreneurial function in modern enterprises. It is an expression of human creativity and imagination by the entire enterprise.

The themes developed earlier can be further developed in terms of the effects of the social system that operates within each organization. The social and political relationships in each workplace and enterprise govern the rate of technological advance, the quality of work produced, the flexibility of its parts (which affects the stability of the whole) and the quality of work life, in the sense of the degree of autonomy and 'self-actualization' achieved by each worker.

Successful workplaces seem to be organized as 'structured chaos' — chaos from dynamic experimentation and autonomy at the grass roots, 'structured' by personal understanding of, and sharing in, the values and purposes of the enterprise. Studies of consumer electronics, aircraft, Chinese reconstruction, Owen's spinning mill in the early nineteenth century, the US telephone industry, Polish producer co-operatives, Philips, Simpson and Mitsubishi in Australia, coal mining in Britain, chemicals, pet-food processing, Saab/Volvo, banking (Citibank) and countless other studies confirm that employee participation, loose structures, shared objectives and 'bottom-up' rather than 'top-down' orientations are successful as principles of organization.

This is particularly important now as people seek expression for post-industrial values, for example 'counting as a person', in the workplace. Semi-autonomous work groups, job enrichment, quality circles, worker participation and similar work innovations are attempts to capture the immense productivity gains inherent in meeting these needs and motivating all the persons in the workplace as a result. Taylor's 'scientific management' approach to task organization is inconsistent with rapid productivity advance in the modern era, as it fails to harness the drive, enthusiasm and entrepreneurial spirit of the workforce.

Appendix: Recommended Research Projects

Here we have brought together (and in many cases elaborated on) the research projects which have been recommended in the course of this book. There are twenty-five of these, although there is some overlap between some of them.

Background projects

1   An update of measures of the 'productivity gaps' between comparable industries in Australia and leading productivity-growth countries, including countries like Taiwan, Singapore and South Korea.

2   The preparation of a substantial publication elucidating both the proximate and fundamental determinants of productivity growth and the policies required to promote that growth.

Impact of government on productivity advance

3   A survey of Australian firms focusing on projects to raise productivity that firms have failed to pursue because of regulations. Such a survey of productivity-inhibiting regulations would reveal which sorts of regulations are problems and which are not. The survey would have to distinguish between short-term impact of regulations and long-term effects that only occur when the firm's behaviour and technology have adjusted.

4   A series of case studies analysing the contribution of regulation/ deregulation to productivity. This study would concentrate on activities which are known to be strongly regulated. The common question in the Brookings Institution study (see page 22) was whether government regulation was achieving its stated objectives, and whether productivity would be enhanced by less regulation or different types of regulation. Parts of an equivalent Australian study could be put together fairly quickly from existing work by Campbell on banking and Davidson on telecommunications, but other industry

case studies would need to be initiated.

5   (a) Studies of the productivity performance of *publicly-owned enterprises* either in comparison with private enterprises in Australia or with similar publicly-owned or private enterprises in other countries; (b) studies of the potential productivity gains *in the public sector* from a greater rate of technological innovation and from adopting different work organization strategies.

6   An investigation of what changes in taxation and subsidies and direct government support would most stimulate overall productivity advance and the number of new products and processes being developed in the economy as a whole.

7   An examination of what changes in the structure of policy-making and in the political system more generally would induce a *longer-term* focus to economic policy conducive to long-term productivity advance, rather than measures for immediate political advantage.

Effects of socio-economic environments on technological change

8   There is a substantial amount of existing data on technology in Australia. If such data from primary and secondary sources were brought together, then the potential use of this data can be reviewed and gaps highlighted.

Data sources already known to us include:

ABS, *Research and Experimental Development, Business Enterprises, Australia* (Cat. 8104.0, 1973–74, 1976–77, 1978–79, 1981–82).

ABS, *Technical Change in Private Non-Farm Enterprises in Australia* (Cat. 8106.0).

ABS, *Research and Experimental Development, Central Government Organisation* (Cat. 8109.0).

ABS, *Foreign Control in Research and Experimental Development, Private Enterprises* (Cat. 5330.0, 1976–77 only).

Bureau of Industry Economics, *Survey of Innovation in Small Manufacturing Firms*, 1980.

Patent, Trade Marks and Design Office, *Official Journal of Patents, Trade Marks and Designs.*

Patent, Trade Marks and Design Office, *Annual Report.*

9   An analysis of research and development in Australia, following on from Stubbs, 1968, 1980; Gannicott (1980). This would include international, inter-industry and inter-firm comparisons of R & D expenditure and inputs. Where the data permit, explaining differences in R & D behaviour in terms of such variables as firm size,

market size, market structure, and other characteristics of firms is suggested. The link between R & D and productivity growth should be investigated. Also, the success of government policies aimed at encouraging R & D could be examined.

10 Patenting activity in Australia. A review of the Australian patent system has recently been carried out by the Industrial Property Advisory Committee. In a recent paper on 'Interpreting Australian Patent Statistics', Simpson (1981) states that 'the review has revived interest in Australian patenting statistics and such opportunities as they may offer to evaluate Australia's position, both *per se* and with respect to other nations'. This paper criticizes earlier work by Stubbs (1968a, 1968b), Encel and Inglis (1966) and Eddington (1976), and suggests that indigenous inventive effort has remained fairly stable over many years and has if anything increased recently. Further investigation into the potential analysis of inventions and innovative activity using patent data is suggested.

11 Diffusion of innovations in Australia. This is a particularly important area for research. The determinants of the rate of diffusion of, say, microprocessors in Australia should be investigated. A comparison of this diffusion process with diffusion in other countries is a particularly promising path. Contact should be made with researchers in this area in other countries to see whether similar diffusion studies are possible, to make the results comparable. Another promising way to investigate the 'specialness' of Australia with respect to the diffusion process, is to investigate the behaviour of multinationals in Australia. Do they adopt new technology in Australia slower or faster than in other countries, and why?

12 A project SAPPHO (see page 33). Given the international importance of project SAPPHO in the evidence about successful innovations, a comparable project in Australia, aimed at highlighting similar causes and influences with special reference to the Australian socio-economic system, could prove very useful.

13 Productivity improvement: a multidisciplinary approach. Project SAPPHO focused on comparing successful and unsuccessful innovations. An alternative approach, placing innovation in a broader context, would be to focus on productivity growth as the central feature to explain. A sample of firms, perhaps from two different industries, could be analysed with respect to their rate of change of productivity. The first could be viewed as possessing a package of characteristics. These would include variables usually included in economic analysis, such as firm size, market size, factor prices, capital intensity, age of capital, R & D expenditure, adoption

of innovations, etc. Other industrial relations, organizational and social characteristics could also be included, however. These could include trade union membership, worker participation, existence of autonomous work groups, labour turnover, amount of lost working time, the regulatory environment, etc. Factor analysis could be used to explain differences in productivity growth.

14   The relationship between static and dynamic efficiency. A central theme of this book has been that the analysis of economic success should be placed in a dynamic context. We need to establish whether attempts to obtain static gains from economies of scale diminish the probability of dynamic gains from innovation. Another area for analysis is the link between investment, the age of capital, and capital utilization. For example, a firm apparently operating efficiently (according to static analysis) may be using outdated capital. Insofar as new technology is embodied in new capital, the level of investment is an important determinant of technological progress. Further, a dynamically efficient firm can be expected to write off its capital relatively quickly because of 'technological obsolescence', which implies a case for relatively high levels of capital utilization (e.g. intensive shift-working) when combining static and dynamic efficiency criteria. Here, any features of the industrial relations and regulatory environment inhibiting intensive capital utilization, may be resisting productivity improvement.

15   The economic environment. We believe that Nelson's point about the relationship between productivity growth and short-run macro-economic performance should be taken seriously. Long-run models of the macro-economy suggest that the higher is productivity growth the lower will be the rate of inflation for a given level of unemployment, or vice versa. However, insofar as productivity growth is induced by demand growth there appear to be short-run macro-economic constraints inhibiting long-run economic growth. Where demand increases, evidence suggests that hours of work respond, but that there is a severe danger of rapid wage inflation following, before sustained employment and sustained growth result. Further research is necessary to investigate how the short-run macro-economic constraints might be overcome to allow the economy to return to a path of low inflation, low unemployment and high productivity growth.

16   Technological change, productivity growth and the labour force. The manpower requirements of technologically progressive firms is an issue worthy of research, and factors contributing to labour mobility would seem worth investigation. On the employment

implications of technological change, the case study approach reviewed earlier is favoured and would possibly be incorporated in research of the type suggested in project 13, above.

Effects of market structures on competitiveness

17 Research into the static and dynamic economies of scale in industrial production processes and into likely future scale economies would be very useful, because it would alert Australian firms to potential productivity gains (and losses) from changes in scale. (See also project 14, above.)

18 The productivity-raising role of cost-efficient transport and communications, within Australia and with our overseas trade partners, could be another extremely useful area of productivity research.

19 A series of case studies of the experiences of Australian firms that have moved successfully into more competitive markets overseas, be it by becoming small multinationals or by establishing themselves as exporters, would be illuminating.

20 A series of case studies:

a intra-industry case studies in Australian industry analysing what makes for productivity leaders and laggards in a given industry;

b international and Australian inter-industry comparisons that highlight the competitive conditions for fast productivity growth in important specific industries;

c historic studies of episodes in which the basis for fast productivity growth was laid: the Meiji period in Japan, the industrial rationalization in Germany after the First World War (industrial standardization, new cost-accounting and management techniques), the productivity push of Taiwan and Singapore in the 1960s, the 'Sichuan experiment' in present-day China.

The organization of work and productivity advance

21 A survey of the managerial literature on enterprises as social systems. The full scope of the *theories* underlying the social system approach must be brought together and made accessible to an Australian audience.

22 A survey of American and European evidence on the dynamic effects on productivity in practice of reorganizing work along social system lines. The Work in America Institute, the National Center on Productivity, and the Research Applied to National Needs Program of the National Science Foundation have all played a key

role in bringing case studies of social system reorganizations of work before an American audience. There is a need for a research programme designed to survey and cull the several hundred American and European case studies, and draw out those cases and practices most appropriate for transplant to Australian conditions. This would not simply be yet another literature survey, but an attempt to pluck from overseas those principles and practices which could be *operational* in this country, and which would lead to organizational structures likely to be dynamic, evolutionary successes in the Australian environment.

23   Analysis of Australian examples of successful social systems reorganizations of workplaces. In Ford's case, for example, where are the details of the changes in work practices? How has productivity altered? Has the quality of working life on the assembly line improved? The details of this case and many like it should be collated, analysed, and publicized. The prodigiously complex nature of the productivity 'equation' suggests that a series of carefully chosen, comparative case studies of this kind be undertaken to investigate the mechanisms by which certain enterprises have forged ahead and others within the same industry have declined. The emphasis should be on isolating social systems structures which yield persistent, evolutionary gains in labour productivity within organizations.

24   A study of company productivity in Japan and the newly-industrializing countries of East and South-East Asia, precisely to see what elements of it could be relevant and useful in Australia.

25   An exploration of what changes in the institutional environment *outside* the enterprise would assist the development of social systems reorganization of enterprises. What difference would the development of industry unions in place of craft unions make? What positive contributions could the union movement and the arbitration authorities make? What government regulations assist or hinder the development of such reorganizations?

References

Abernathy, W.J. & Townsend, P.L. (1975), 'Technology, productivity and process change', *Technological forecasting and social change* 7, 4, pp. 379-96.

Addison, J.T. & Barnett, A.M. (1982), 'The Impact of Unions on Productivity', *British Journal of Industrial Relations* 3, 2, pp. 145-62.

Alber, A.F. (1979), 'The real cost of job enrichment', *Business Horizons* 22, 1.

Alexander, K.O. (1983), 'The Changing American Workplace', *Technology Review* 13, November/December.

Amato, L., Ryan, J.M. & Wilder, R.P. (1981), 'Market Structure and Dynamic Performance in US Manufacturing', *Southern Economic Journal* 47, 4, pp. 1105-10.

Aubrey, H.G. (1955), 'Industrial Investment Decisions : A Comparative Analysis', *Journal of Economic History*, December, pp. 335-51.

Baumol, W.J. (1968), 'Entrepreneurship in Economic Theory', *American Economic Review*, Supplement (May), pp. 64-71.

Birchall, D. & Wild, R. (1973), 'Job Restructuring Amongst Blue-Collar Workers', *Personnel Review*, Spring.

Bjorn-Anderson, N. & Hedberg, B.L.T. (1977), 'Designing information systems in an organizational perspective', *North Holland/TIMS Studies in the Management Sciences* 5.

Boretsky, M. (1980), 'The Role of Innovation', *Challenge* 23, 5, pp. 9-15.

Bosworth, D.L. (1983a), *Statistics of Invention*, Pergamon.

Bosworth, D.L. (1983b), 'Recent Developments in the Economics of Technological Change Literature', *Economics*, Autumn.

Bosworth, D. & Wilson, R. (1980), 'Returns to Scale in R. & D. Empirical Evidence from the World Chemical Industry', Discussion Paper No. 80, CIEBR, University of Warwick, Coventry.

Bowles, S., Gordon, D.M. & Weisskopf, T.E. (1984), 'A Social Model for U.S. Productivity Growth', *Challenge* 27, 1, pp. 41-8.

Brown, C. & Medoff, J. (1978), 'Trade Unions in the Production Process', *Journal of Political Economy* 86, 3, pp. 355-78.

Burns, T. and Stalker, G.M. (1961), *The Management of Innovation*, Tavistock, London.

Butcher, W.C. (1979), 'Closing our "Production Gap"; Key to US Economic Health', *Industrial Engineering* 11, 12, pp. 30-3.

Byrnes, M. (1984), 'The Japan Connection: Long Overdue for a Total Overhaul', *Australian Financial Review*, Monday 27 August, p. 11.

Byrt, W.J. & Masters, P.R. (1974), *The Australian Manager*, Sun Books, Melbourne.

Cable, J.R. & Fitzroy, F.R. (1980), 'Productive efficiency, incentives and employee

Structured Chaos

participation: some preliminary results for West Germany', *Kyklos* 33, 1, pp. 100–21.

Caves, R.E. (1980), 'Productivity differences among industries' in *Britain's Economic Performance*, Caves and Krause (eds), Brookings, Washington.

Caves, D.W. and Christensen, L.R. (1980), 'The Relative Efficiency of Public and Private Firms in a competitive environment: the case of Canadian railroads', *Journal of Political Economy*, 88, 5, pp. 958–76.

Caves, D.W., Christensen, L.R. & Swanson, J.A. (1981), 'Economic performance in regulated and unregulated environments; a comparison of US and Canadian railroads', *Quarterly Journal of Economics* 96, 4, pp. 559–81.

Caves, D.W., Christensen, L.R. & Tretheway, M.W. (1982), 'Airline Productivity under Deregulation', *Regulation* 6, 6, pp. 25–8.

Chi-Liang Yang (1981), '"Mass line" accounting in China', *Management Accounting* 62, 11, pp. 13–17.

Collins, E.L. (1981), 'Tax Incentives for Innovation — Productivity Miracle or Media Hype?', *Journal of Post-Keynesian Economics* 4, 1, pp. 68–74.

Crombie, A. (1976), 'Industrial democracy — job satisfaction or social transformation', in R.L. Pritchard (ed.) *Industrial Democracy in Australia*, CCH Australia, Sydney.

Cummings, T.G. & Molloy, E.S. (1977), *Improving Productivity and the Quality of Work Life*, Praeger, New York.

Denison, E.F. (1967), *Why Growth Rates Differ*, Brookings Institution, Washington.

Dymmel, M.D. (1979), 'Technology in telecommunications: its effect on labour and skills', *Monthly Labour Review* 102, 1, pp. 13–19.

Eads, G.C. (1980), 'Innovation, Technological Progress and Research and Development, Regulation and Technical Change: Some Largely Unexplored Influences', *American Economic Review* 70, 2.

Eddington, I.W. (1976), Patents, M.Ec. thesis, University of Queensland.

Edwards, P.K. & Nolan, P. (1983), Industrial relations, productivity, and economic performance: an outline of the connections, unpublished paper, University of Warwick, Coventry.

Elbaum, B. & Wilkinson, F. (1979), 'Industrial relations and uneven development: a comparative study of the American and British steel industries', *Cambridge Journal of Economics* 3, pp. 275–303.

Emery, F.E. & Phillips, C.R. (1976), *Living at Work*, AGPS, Canberra.

Encel, S. & Inglis, A. (1966), 'Patents, Inventions and Economic Progress', *Economic Record* 42, pp. 572–88.

England, G.W. (1975), *The Manager and His Values: An International Perspective*, Ballinger Press, Cambridge, Mass.

Ettlie, J.E. and Vellenga, D.B. (1979), 'Adoption Time Period for some Transport Innovations', *Management Science* 25, May.

Ford, G.W. & Hearn, J.W. (1980), 'Industrial Conflict: an overview' in Ford, Hearn & Lansbury (eds), *Australian Labour Relations*, Macmillan, Melbourne.

Ford, G.W. (1982), 'Human Resource Development in Australia and the Balance of Skills', *Journal of Industrial Relations*, September.

Ford, G.W. (1983), 'Cultural Difference in Skill Formation and the Establishment of an Australian Human Resource Office', *Manpower Planning and Industrial Development in Uncertain Times*, ANZAAS, Sydney.

Freeman, C. (1971), *The Role of Small Firms in Innovation in the United Kingdom Since 1945*, Report to the Bolton Committee of Enquiry on Small Firms, Research Report No. 6, HMSO, London.

Freeman, C. (1982), *The Economics of Industrial Innovation*, 2nd edition, Frances Pinter, London.

Freeman, R.B. & Medoff, J.L. (1979), 'The Two Faces of Unionism', *The Public Interest* 57, Fall, pp. 69–93.

Gannicott, K.G. (1980), 'Research and Development Incentives' in *Technological Change in Australia* 4. Report of the Committee of Inquiry into Technological Change in Australia.

Gibson, T.A. (1976), 'Technology transfer and economic progress', *Business Economics* 11, 3, pp. 23–30.

Gillett, D. & Ashkenas, R.N. (1981), 'Hard times? Manage results, not just resources', *SAM Advanced Management Journal* 46, 4, pp. 4–12.

Globerman, S. & Smart, C. (1983), 'The outlook for productivity growth in the 1980s', *Cost and Management* 57, 5, pp. 4–9.

Gollop, F.M. & Roberts, M.J. (1983), 'Environmental regulations and productivity growth; the case of fossil-fueled electric power generation', *Journal of Political Economy* 91, 4, pp. 654–74.

Gunzburg, D. (1979), 'Industrial Democracy in Australia'. Report for the ILO, Department of Science and Technology, Melbourne.

Hackman, J. & Lawler, E. (1971), 'Employee Reactions to Job Characteristics', *Journal of Applied Psychology*, June.

Hackman, J.R. & Oldham, G.R. (1980), *Work Redesign*, Addison-Wesley, Massachusetts.

Hackman, J., Oldham, G., Janson, R. & Purdy, K. (1975), 'A New Strategy for Job Enrichment', *California Management Review*, Summer.

Hagen, E.E. (1962), *On the Theory of Social Change: How Economic Growth Begins*, Irwin, Homewood, Illinois.

Hamberg, D. (1966), *R & D: Essays in the Economics of Industrial Innovation*, Random House, New York.

Hanlon, M.D. (1981), 'Public Sector Productivity in an era of retrenchment', *National Productivity Review* 1, 1, pp. 100–09.

Herzberg, F., Mausner, B. & Snyderman, B. (1959), *The Motivation to Work*, Wiley, New York.

Herzberg, F. (1966), *Work and the Nature of Man*, World Publishing, Cleveland.

Hirschmann, A.O. (1958), *The Strategy of Economic Development*, Yale University Press, New Haven.

Hirschmeier, J. (1964), *The Origins of Entrepreneurship in Meiji Japan*, Harvard University Press, Cambridge, Massachusetts.

Jewkes, J., Sawers, D. & Stelleman, R. (1969), *The Sources of Invention*, W.W. Norton, New York.

Johnson, C.M. & Pikarsky, M. (1984), Towards Fragmentation: The Evolution of Public Transportation in Chicago. Unpublished paper by Johnson (Director of Research, American Public Works Association) and Pikarsky (Director of Research, Illinois Institute of Technology Research Institute).

Jones, D.C. (1983), 'The Economic Performance of Producer Cooperatives Within Command Economies: Evidence for the Case of Poland', Working Paper, Department of Economics, Hamilton College, Clinton, New York.

Kain, P.G. (1981), Urban Transport Crisis. A Study of Adelaide Bus Operations in Transition, 1967–1981. Unpublished thesis, Flinders University of South Australia.

Kamien, M. and Schwartz, N. (1975), 'Market Structure and Innovative Activity: A Survey', *Journal of Economic Literature* 13, pp. 1–37.

Kasper, W. (1980), 'Technological Change and Economic Growth' in *Technological Change in Australia Vol. 4*, Report of the Committee of Inquiry into Technological Change in Australia.

Kasper, W., Blandy, R., et al. (1980), *Australia at the Crossroads — Our Choices to the Year 2000*, Harcourt Brace, Sydney–New York.

Kasper, W. and Masih, A. (1979), 'Apparent Productivity in Australian Industries: An International Comparison', *Australian Bulletin of Labour* 6, 1, pp. 52–61.

Kaspura, A. and Ho-Trieu, L. (1980), 'Productivity and Technological Change in Australian 3-Digit Manufacturing Industries 1968–9 to 1977–78', Department of Productivity Research Branch, Working Paper No. 10.

Kendrick, J. (1977), *Understanding Productivity*, Johns Hopkins University Press, Baltimore.

Kendrick, J. and Grossman, E. (1980), *Productivity in the United States*, Johns Hopkins University Press, Baltimore.

Klein, B.H. (1977), *Dynamic Economics*, Harvard University Press, Cambridge, Massachusetts.

Kriegler, R.J. (1980), *Working for the Company*, Oxford University Press, Melbourne.

Kriegler, R.J. and Sloan, J. (1984), 'Technological change and migrant employment', Working Paper Series, No. 62, National Institute of Labour Studies, Adelaide.

Kriegler, R.J. (1984), *Japanese Personnel Practices at Mitsubishi Australia*, Working Paper Series, No. 71, National Institute of Labour Studies, Adelaide.

Lansbury, R.D. and Spillane, R. (1983), *Organizational Behaviour: The Australian Context*, Longman Cheshire, Melbourne.

Lazonick, W.H. (1979), 'Industrial relations and technical change: the case of the self-acting mule', *Cambridge Journal of Economics* 3, pp. 231–62.

Lazonick, W.H. (1981), 'Production Relations, Labour Productivity, and Choice of Technique: British and U.S. Cotton Spinning', *The Journal of Economic History* 41, September, pp. 491–516.

Leibenstein, H. (1968), 'Entrepreneurship and Development', *American Economic Review (Papers and Proceedings)* 58, May, pp. 72–83.

Lenski, G.E. (1966), *Power and Privilege: A Theory of Stratification*, McGraw-Hill, New York.

Lindbeck, A. (1981), 'Industrial Policy as an Issue in the Economic Environment', *The World Economy*, December, pp. 391–405.

Lindner, R., Fischer, A. and Pardey, P. (1979), 'The Time to Adoption', *Economic Letters* 2, pp. 187–90.

Lydall, H. (1980), 'Technological Change and Economic Growth' in *Technological Change in Australia Vol. 4*, Report of the Committee of Inquiry into Technological Change in Australia.

McCain, R.A. (1978), 'Endogenous bias in technical progress and environmental policy', *American Economic Review*, 68, 4, pp. 538–46.

McClelland, D. (1961), *The Achieving Society*, D. Van Nostrand, New York.

McClelland, D. et al. (1969), *Motivating Economic Achievement*, Free Press, New York.

Malkiel, B.G. (1979), 'Productivity — the problem behind the headlines', *Harvard Business Review* 57, 3, pp. 81–91.

Mansfield, E. (1968), *The Economics of Technological Change*, W.W. Norton, New York.

Mansfield, E. et al. (1981), 'Imitation Costs and Patents: An Empirical Study', *Economic Journal* 91, pp. 907–18.

Marshall, A. (1920), *Principles of Economics*, Macmillan, London (eighth edition, 1961).

Mescon, T.S. and Vozikis, G.S. (1982), 'Federal regulation; What are the costs?',

Business, the magazine of managerial thought and action 32, 1, pp. 33–9.

Metcalfe, J.S. and Hall, P.H. (1983), 'The Verdoorn Law and the Salter Mechanism: A Note on Australian Manufacturing Industry', *Australian Economic Papers*, December.

Muller, B. (1980), 'Bureaucracy, job control and militancy', in S. Frenkel (ed.), *Industrial Action*, George Allen & Unwin, Sydney.

Myers, D.D. (1983), 'Technical Entrepreneurship and Revitalization', *Engineering Management International* 1, 4, pp. 275–80.

Nasbeth, L. and Ray, G.F. (1974), *The Diffusion of New Industrial Processes: An International Study*, Cambridge University Press, Cambridge.

Nelson, R.A. and Wohar, M.E. (1983), 'Regulation, Scale Economies, and Productivity in Steam-Electric Generation', *International Economic Review* 24, 1, pp. 57–79.

Nelson, R.R. (1981), 'Research on productivity growth and productivity differences: dead ends and new departures', *Journal of Economic Literature* 19, 3, pp. 1029–64.

Nelson, R.R., and Winter, S.G. (1977), 'In search of useful theory of innovation', *Research Policy* 6, 1, pp. 36–76.

Nevis, E.C. (1983), 'Cultural assumptions and productivity; the United States and China', *Sloan Management Review* 24, 3, pp. 17–29.

Nickell, S. (1978), *The Investment Decision of Firms*, Cambridge University Press and Nisbet, Welwyn Garden City.

Norris, W.K. (1976), 'Manpower Aspects of Technical Progress', *International Journal of Social Economics* 3, 2, pp. 74–88.

OECD (1983), *Positive Adjustment Policies*, OECD, Paris.

Olson, M. (1984), 'Why Nations Rise and Fall' (interview), *Challenge* 27, 1, pp. 15–23.

Papenek, G.P. (1962), 'The Development of Entrepreneurship', *American Economic Review*, May, pp. 45–58.

Peek, M.J. (1962), 'Inventions in the Post-War American Aluminium Industry' in R.R. Nelson (ed.), *The Rate and Direction of Inventive Activity, Economic and Social Factors*, Princeton University Press, pp. 279–98.

Penrose, E.T. (1959), *The Theory of the Growth of the Firm*, Basil Blackwell, Oxford.

Peters, E.B. (1978), 'Job security, technical innovation and productivity', *Personnel Journal* 57, 1, pp. 32–5.

Peters, T.J. and Waterman, R.H. (1983), *In Search of Excellence: Lessons from America's Best-Run Companies*, Warner Books, New York.

Phelps-Brown, H. (1977), 'What is the British Predicament?', *Three Banks Review,* 116, December.

Phillips, A. (1975), *Promoting Competition in Regulated Markets*, The Brookings Institution, Washington.

Piekarz, R. (1983), 'R & D and Productivity Growth: Studies and Issues', *American Economic Review (Papers and Proceedings)* 73, 2, pp. 210–14.

Prais, S.J. (1981), *Productivity and Industrial Structure*, Cambridge University Press, Cambridge.

Pratten, C.F. (1976), *Labour Productivity Differentials within International Companies*, Cambridge University Press, Cambridge.

Pym, D.L. (1971), 'Social change in the business firm', in D. Mills (ed.), *Australian Management and Society*, Penguin, Melbourne.

Ranftl, R.M., Togna, A.D. and Stahl, M.J. (1977), 'Improving R and D productivity', *Research Management* 20, 1, pp. 25–9.

Reekie, W.D. (1979), *Industry, Prices and Markets*, Philip Allan, Oxford.

Robertson, D. (1978), 'Australia's Growth performance: an assessment' in
    Kasper and Parry (eds), *Growth Trade and Structural Change in an Open
    Australian Economy*, University of New South Wales, Centre for Applied
    Economic Research, Sydney.
Rosenberg, N. (1974), 'Science, Invention and Economic Growth', *Economic Jour-
    nal* 84, pp. 90–108.
Rosenbloom, R.S. and Abernathy, W.J. (1982), 'The climate for innovation in
    industry', *Research Policy* 11, 4, pp. 209–25.
Rosow, J.M. (1979), 'People and the productivity equation', *Journal of Contempor-
    ary Business* 8, 4.
Sahal, D. (1983), 'Technology, Productivity and Industry Structure', *Technological
    Forecasting and Social Change* 24, 1, pp. 1–13.
Salomon, J.J. (1980), 'Technical change and economic policy', *OECD Observer*
    104, May.
Salter, W.E.G. (1966), *Productivity and Technical Change*, Cambridge University
    Press, Cambridge.
Scherer, F.M. (1982), 'Demand-Pull and Technological Innovation. Schmookler
    Revisited', *Journal of Industrial Economics* 30, 3, pp. 225–38.
Scherer, F.M. (1983), 'Concentration, R & D, and Productivity Change', *Southern
    Economic Journal* 50, 1.
Schmookler, J. (1966), *Invention and Economic Growth*, Harvard University
    Press, Cambridge, Massachusetts.
Schultze, C.L. (1983), 'Industrial Policy: A Dissent', *The Brookings Review* 2,
    Fall, pp. 3–12.
Schumpeter, J. (1934), *The Theory of Economic Development,* Harvard Univer-
    sity Press, Cambridge, Massachusetts.
Sentry Holdings (1978), *Managers and Workers at the Crossroads*, Harbour
    Press, Sydney.
Sentry Holdings (1981), *Perspectives on Productivity: Australia,* Harbour Press,
    Sydney.
Shimonshi, D. (1970), 'The mobile scientist in the American instrument indus-
    try', *Minerva* 8, 1, pp. 59–89.
Simpson, B.J. (1981), 'Interpreting Australian Patent Statistics', Economic Society
    of Australia and New Zealand, New South Wales Branch, Economic Mono-
    graph No. 360.
Srivastva, S. et al. (1975), *Job Satisfaction and Productivity*, Case Western
    Reserve, Cleveland.
Stoneman, P. (1981), 'Intra Firm Diffusion, Bayesian Learning and Profitability',
    Economic Journal 91, pp. 375–88.
Stoneman, P. (1983), *The Economic Analysis of Technological Change*, Oxford
    University Press, Oxford.
Stubbs, P. (1968a), *Innovation and Research, A Study in Australian Industry,*
    F.W. Cheshire for Institute of Applied Economic Research, University of
    Melbourne.
Stubbs, P. (1968b), 'Australia's Economic Performance in Patent Applications: A
    Comment', *Economic Record* 44, pp. 113–15.
Stubbs, P. (1980), *Technology and Australia's Future: Industry and International
    Competitiveness*, Australian Industry Development Association Research
    Centre.
Swann, K. (1975), 'Management of small business', *Production engineer* 54, 1,
    pp. 25–33.
Tacy, L. and Gough, R. (1982), 'Technological change — its impact on organiza-

tions and jobs'. Paper delivered at the Australian and New Zealand Association for the Advancement of Science, Macquarie University.

Terleckyj, N.E. (1980), 'What do R & D Numbers tell us about technological change?', *American Economic Review* 70, 2, pp. 55–61.

Townsend, J. et al. (1982), *Innovations in Britain since 1945*, Science Policy Research Unit, Occasional Working Paper No. 16, University of Sussex.

Trist, E. and Bamforth, K. (1951), 'Some Social and Psychological Consequences of the Longwall Method Coal Getting', *Human Relations*, February.

Trist, E., Higgin, G., Murray, H. and Pollock, A. (1963), *Organisational Choice*, Tavistock, London.

Walters, R. (1982), 'The Citibank Project: Improving Productivity through Work Redesign', in Zager, R. and Rosow, M. (eds), *The Innovative Organisation*, Pergamon, New York.

Wang, K. (1974), 'Worker participation matrix', *Personnel Practice Bulletin* 30, 3, September.

Weber, M. (1948), *The Protestant Ethic and the Spirit of Capitalism*, Allen & Unwin, London.

Weisskopf, T.E., Bowles, S. and Gordon, D.M. (1983), 'Hearts and Minds: A Social Model of U.S. Productivity Growth', *Brookings Papers on Economic Activity* 2, pp. 381–450.

Willis, R. (1984), Speech to Department of Employment and Industrial Relations seminar on industrial democracy and employee participation. Melbourne, 17 August.

Wilson, B. (1982), 'A progressive strategy for employee relations', *Management decision* 20, 5/6.

Yamamura, K. (1968), 'A Re-examination of Entrepreneurship in Meiji Japan (1868–1912)', *Economic History Review*, February, pp. 148–58.

Yankelovich, D. and Immerwahr, J. (1983), 'The emergence of expressivism will revolutionize the contract between workers and employers', *Personnel Administrator* 28, 12, pp. 34–9, 114.

Index

Abernathy, W.J., 27, 62
Addison, J.T., 65
Alber, A.F., 75
Alexander, K.O., 71
Ashkenas, R.N., 64
Aubrey, H.G., 56
Australian Telecommunications
Employees Association (ATEA),
84

Barnett, A.M., 65
Baumol, W.J., 56
'Bayesian learning' models, see
technological change
Birchall, D., 81
Bjorn-Anderson, N., 84
Boretsky, M., 24
Bosworth, D.L., 27, 29–30
Bowles, S., 6, 56
Brookings Institution, 22, 95
Brown, C., 65
Burns, T., 11
Butcher, W.C., 20
Byrnes, M., 8–9
Byrt, W.J., 70

Cable, J.R., 65
Campbell, —, 95
Cantillon, R., 55
Caves, D.W., 20, 23
Caves, R.E., 67
Chi-Liang Yang, 64
Christensen, L.R., 20, 23
Citibank experiment, see workplace
organization
Collins, E.L., 24
Committee of Inquiry into
Technological Change in Australia,
42
competitiveness: costs, 47–8; dynamic

approach, 47, 49, 92;
entrepreneurial activities, 10, 48;
government intervention, 9–10,
49–50, 57–8, 92; macrostability and
microstability, 57, 61; market
niche, 47–51, 57, 80, 92; 'night cap'
competition, 48; price, 47–8;
production costs, 1, 4; risks, 56–8;
rivalry, 20, 47–51, 92–3;
technological change, 10, 22, 43,
48, 51, 57, 92; trade unions, 65;
United Kingdom, 65; wages, 4
Crombie, A., 75
Cummings, T.G., 76, 78, 81

Davidson, —, 95
Denison, E.F., 14
Department of Science and
Technology (C'wealth), 87
diffusion, see technological change
Dymmel, M.D., 64

Eads, G.C., 39
economic growth, 1–3, 6–7, 24,
42, 46, 59
economies of scale, 8, 17, 19, 22, 46,
49–50, 85, 87, 93
Eddington, I.W., 97
Edwards, P.K., 67–9
efficiency, dynamic and static, 10–14,
29, 43, 45
Elbaum, B., 65
Emery, F.E., 71
Encel, S., 97
England, G.W., 69–70
entrepreneurial activities: Australia,
56, 59; competitiveness and, 10,
48; definition, 54, 93; diffusion
and, 35; government regulations,
20–1, 59; productivity, 54–5, 59;

R & D, 28, 30, 33; role and
concerns, 21, 48, 52–9, 92–3;
see also technological change;
workplace organization
environment, 10, 28
Ettlie, J.E., 11

Fischer, A., 35
Fitzroy, F.R., 65
Ford, G.W., 69, 82
Freeman, C., 31–4
Freeman, R.B., 65

Gannicott, K.G., 42, 45, 96
Gibson, T.A., 27
Gillett, D., 64
Globerman, S., 23
Gollop, F.M., 20
Gordon, D.M., 6, 56
Gough, R., 84
government regulations and
intervention: affirmative action,
18; Australia, 19, 21–3; Canada, 20;
competitiveness, 9–10, 49–50,
57–8, 92; cost and adverse effect
of, 9–10, 18–21; environmental,
18–19; health and safety, 18–19; as
'insurance', 9–10; occupational, 18;
and productivity, 9–10, 12, 16,
18–25, 39, 91–2; R & D, 20, 39;
sunrise and sunset legislation, 20;
technological change, 21–4, 39;
United States, 20, 22, 24
Grossman, E., 15n
Gunzburg, D., 72

Hackman, J.R., 81–2
Hagen, E.E., 54–6
Hall, P.H., 44
Hamberg, D., 30
Hanlon, M.D., 23
Hearn, J.W., 69
Hedberg, B.L.T., 84
Herzberg, F., 80–2
Herzberg-Hackman theory, *see*
workplace organization
Hirschmann, A.O., 56
Hirschmeier, J., 54
Ho-Trieu, L., 44

Immerwahr, J., 73
income, 2–4, 91
Industrial Property Advisory

Committee, 97
Inglis, A., 97
innovation, *see* technological change
invention, *see* technological change

Jewkes, J., 29–31
jobs, 1–2, 21
Johnson, C.M., 21–2
Jones, D.C., 65

Kain, P.G., 23
Kamien, M., 29–30
Kasper, W., 3n, 42–3, 59
Kaspura, A., 44
Kendrick, J., 14, 15n, 16
Klein, B.H., 6, 10–11, 25, 50, 52, 57–8
Kriegler, R.J., 83

labour force, 18, 36, 38–41, 44, 46,
72–3, 82–3; *see also* technological
change; workplace organization
Lansbury, R.D., 71
Lawler, E., 81
Leibenstein, H., 56
Lenski, G.E., 69
Lindbeck, A., 47
Lindner, R., 35
living standards, 1, 13, 42
Lydall, H., 42

McCain, R.A., 20
McClelland, D., 55
macrostability and microstability, *see*
competitiveness
Malkiel, B.G., 20, 24
Mansfield, E., 28–31, 35
Mansfield 'epidemic approach', *see*
technological change
manufacturing, 3–4, 44; *see also*
workplace organization
Marshall, A., 7, 12
Marx, K., 55
Masih, A., 3n
Masters, P.R., 70
Medoff, J.L., 65
Mescon, T.S., 20, 57
Metcalfe, J.S., 44
Mitsubishi Motors Co., *see* workplace
organization
Molloy, E.S., 76, 78, 81
monopoly, 49–50, 93
Muller, B., 84
Myers, D.D., 28, 50

Nasbeth, L., 35–6, 37n
National Institute of Labour Studies, 87
Nelson, R.A., 6, 20
Nelson, R.R., 6, 26–8, 36, 38–40, 67, 98
Nevis, E.C., 50
Nolan, P., 67–9
Norris, W.K., 57

Organisation for Economic Co-operation and Development (OECD), 2n, 41–2
organizational progress: definition, 26
Ortega y Gasset, J., 21
Owen's spinning mill, *see* workplace organization

Papanek, G.P., 56
Pardey, P., 35
patenting activity, *see* technological change
Peek, M.J., 30
Peters, E.B., 64
Peters, T.J., 6–7, 25, 34, 50, 54, 56, 62
Phelps-Brown, Sir Henry, 6
Philips Co., *see* workplace organization
Phillips, A., 19
Phillips, C.R., 71
Piekarz, R., 27
Pikarsky, M., 21–2
Prais, S.J., 67
Pratten, C.F., 67
productivity: Australia, 1–5, 12, 19, 22–3, 44–5, 49–52, 54–5, 59, 72, 91–3; Canada, 20, 23, 91; capital productivity, 13; China, 64; comparisons, 1, 3, 23; competitiveness and, 1; decline, 6, 22–5, 27, 65, 72; definition, 12–14, 91; determinants, 13–16; dynamic approach, 5, 9–11, 52, 89; government regulations, 9–10, 12, 16, 18–25, 39, 91–2; growth, 2, 4–6, 9, 11–12, 14–18, 24–8, 36, 38–41, 44–5, 51–2, 54–5, 59, 64–6, 91–2; Hong Kong, 1; income and, 4; Japan, 1, 8–9; labour productivity, 13; living standards, 1, 13; production costs, 1; production function, 14; productivity gap, 4; productivity

underhang, 4, 91; public sector, 23; R & D, 28, 36, 45; 'residual' or 'third factor', 14; Salter mechanism, 44; social arrangements, 2, 4–9, 16–17, 22–3, 36, 38, 61, 64–7, 91; technological change, 23, 26–7, 36, 38, 41, 44–5; total factor productivity, 13–14; trade unions, 64–5; unemployment, 41; United States, 3–4, 6–7, 15–16, 18, 20, 22–3, 27, 65, 91–2; Verdoorn law, 44; West Germany, 3–4
Pym, D.L., 69

Ranftl, R.M., 62, 63n
Ray, G.F., 35–6, 37n
Reekie, W.D., 35
research and development (R & D): Australia, 41–2, 45, 92; comparisons, 41; expenditure, 27–30, 36, 41–2; by government, 28, 42n; government regulations, 20, 39; by private industry, 20, 42n; productivity and, 28, 36, 45; size of firm, 28–34, 92; United Kingdom, 41; United States, 20, 27, 41; *see also* technological change
research projects, recommended, 4, 23–5, 45–6, 52, 59–60, 88–90, 95–100
Roberts, M.J., 20
Robertson, D., 42
Rosenberg, N., 30
Rosenbloom, R.S., 62
Rosow, J.M., 66

'S-shaped' diffusion curve, *see* technological change
Saab-Scandia Co., *see* workplace organization
Sahal, D., 24, 28
Salomon, J.J., 24, 27
Salter, W.E.G., 35
Salter mechanism, *see* productivity
SAPPHO project, 33–4, 45, 97
Say, J.B., 55
Scherer, F.M., 28, 30
Schmookler, J., 29–30
Schmooklerian hypothesis, 30; *see also* technological change
Schultze, C.L., 25

Schumpeter, J., 35, 55
'Schumpeter approach', *see*
    technological change
Schwartz, N., 30
Sentry Holdings Ltd, 70
Shimonshi, D., 32, 33n, 34
Simpson, B.J., 97
Simpson Holdings Ltd, *see* workplace
    organization
Sloan, J., 83
Smart, C., 23
Spillane, R., 71
Spurling, G., 83
Srivastva, S., 78
Stalker, G.M., 11
'stock adjustment approach', *see*
    technological change
Stoneman, P., 26, 29-30, 35
Stubbs, P., 41, 42n, 43-5, 96-7
Swann, K., 51
Swanson, J.A., 20

Tacy, L., 84
Tavistock Institute of Human
    Relations, 76, 80
Taylor, F., 65
Taylorism, *see* workplace organization
technological change: Australia, 41-6,
    83-6, 91; competitiveness and, 10,
    22, 43, 48, 51, 57, 92; definition,
    26, 29; de-skilling, 41, 72, 82-3;
    diffusion and its innovations
    theory, 26-8, 34-7, 45, 92; dynamic
    approaches, 11, 45-6; government
    regulations, 21-4, 39; innovations,
    10-11, 21-3, 26-34, 39, 41, 43, 45,
    48, 51, 57, 91-2; input measure
    (expenditure on R & D), 27-30,
    36; inventions, 26-31, 34-5, 45,
    92; Japan, 43, 64; labour force, 36,
    38-41, 44, 46; living standards and,
    42; output measure (patenting
    activity), 27-30, 34, 41, 45, 92;
    productivity and, 23, 26-7, 36, 38,
    41, 44-5; social arrangements and,
    10-12, 23, 43, 64, 84-6; United
    Kingdom, 43; United States, 21-2,
    24, 43; West Germany, 43
Terleckyj, N.E., 27-8
Townsend, J., 31n
Townsend, P.L., 27
trade unions, 64-5, 67-8, 70-1, 84
Tretheway, M.W., 20

Trist, E., 76, 80

unemployment, 4, 41, 43-4, 71

Vellenga, D.B., 11
Verdoorn law, *see* productivity
'vintage approach', *see* technological
    change
Volvo Co., *see* workplace organization
Vozikis, G.S., 20, 57
wages, *see* income
Walters, R., 82
Walton, R., 78-9
Wang, K., 76, 77n
Waterman, R.H., 6-7, 25, 34, 50, 54,
    56, 62
Weber, M., 55
Weisskopf, T.E., 6, 56
Wild, R., 81
Wilkinson, F., 65
Willis, R., 11-12
Wilson, B., 68
Wilson, R., 30
Winter, S.G., 27-8
Wohar, M.E., 20
workplace organization: Australia, 61,
    69-75, 83-9; Australian manager
    and employee profiles, 70-3, 83;
    China, 64, 93; Citibank
    experiment, 82, 93; comparisons,
    70, 78; conflicts and polarization,
    68-9, 71-2, 76, 83-5; dynamic
    approaches, 7-12, 50-1, 61, 64, 68,
    94; entrepreneurial activities, 52-6,
    94; Herzberg-Hackman theory,
    80-2; Japan, 64, 70, 88-90;
    Mitsubishi Motors Co., 73, 83, 93;
    Owen's spinning mill, 64, 93;
    Philips Co., 73-5, 93; Poland, 65,
    93; quality of work-life, 61, 72, 80,
    93; Saab-Scandia Co., 79, 93;
    Simpson Holdings Ltd., 85-7, 93;
    Taylorism, 66, 72, 78, 94; trade
    unions, 65, 67-8, 71, 84; United
    Kingdom, 64, 67, 70, 76-8, 93;
    United States, 61, 64-6, 70, 75,
    78-9, 82, 93; Volvo Co., 79-80, 93;
    West Germany, 65; workers'
    involvement, 6-8, 16, 61-4, 66-9,
    71-89, 93-4.

Yamamura, K., 54
Yankelovich, D., 73